Additional books written by Richard Paul and Linda Elder:

Critical Thinking: Tools for Taking Charge of Your Professional and Personal Life

Critical Thinking: Tools for Taking Charge of Your Learning and Your Life, 3rd edition

Critical Thinking: Learn the Tools the Best Thinkers Use

The Thinkers Guide series written by Richard Paul and Linda Elder titles includes:

Critical Thinking: Concepts and Tools

Analytic Thinking: How to Take Thinking Apart and What to Look for When You Do

How to Detect Media Bias and Propaganda in National and World News

Fallacies: The Art of Mental Trickery and Manipulation

Taking Charge of the Human Mind

How to Read a Paragraph: The Art of Close Reading

How to Write a Paragraph: The Art of Substantive Writing

Understanding the Foundations of Ethical Reasoning

The Art of Asking Essential Questions

Also written by Richard Paul:

Critical Thinking: How to Survive in a Rapidly Changing World

D1166081

More on What People Say About the *30 Days* Book...

"In their book, 30 *Days to Better Thinking and Better Living Through Critical Thinking*, Dr. Linda Elder and Dr. Richard Paul provide nothing less than a psychological GPS system for mental clarity. If you're serious about living according to your true intentions, then you must develop a capacity for critically thinking about what you think. At first blush, 'thinking about what you think' may sound like a Zen Koan—don't be intimidated. With practical, incremental guidelines for challenging destructive, self-deceptive habits, beliefs, and vague thinking, you will be experiencing your world in vivid, HD clarity in just 30 days. If you've ever dreamt about being more effective, more balanced, and more content with life, follow this step-by-step program. It's amazing!"

—Dr. Joe Luciani, Bestselling Author of *Self-Coaching: The Powerful Program to Beat Anxiety and Depression*

"It is ironic and in many ways tragic that you can go through 12 years of undergraduate education, 4 years of college, and 4–6 years of graduate school, and still never learn how to think. Educators mouth the words 'critical thinking,' but in my 35 years as a college professor, writer, and public intellectual, I have found that almost no one knows how to think. They may know *what* to think if they are good at memorization, but the all important skill of learning *how* to think is still a lost art. This makes the work of Dr. Linda Elder and Dr. Richard Paul vital to the progress of our democratic society, and 30 *Days to Better Thinking and Better Living Through Critical Thinking* is their best guide yet on teaching people how to think, not just about *big ideas*, but about everything in life. Buy this book, change your life, and in the process make the world a safer and saner place to live."

—Dr. Michael Shermer, Publisher of *Skeptic* magazine; Author of *Why People Believe Weird Things*

"One of the qualities that sets us apart from thinking creatures of other species is our ability—if we choose to use it—to 'think about our thinking.' My husband, the pioneering psychologist, humanist, and great thinker: Albert Ellis, Ph.D., would remind people of that fact, tirelessly and constantly! In this substantial, clear, and easy-to-read book by Dr. Linda Elder and Dr. Richard Paul . . . readers are offered stimulating descriptions, definitions, principles, and suggestions for understanding and using thinking in effective ways in order to experience a better quality of life. The earnest dedication of the authors to contributing impactful ideas—and to encouraging their readers to allow themselves to experience growth in their lives through making choices to think and act in beneficial ways—is felt strongly throughout the whole book. That in itself is inspiring to read and feel. The topic is presented through combining the premises and ideas of the authors with guidelines which allow us to identify problematic flaws in thinking in order that we may prevent such flaws, along with action strategies—indeed fine exercise for the mind and the brain. Additionally it is uplifting to read the urging of the authors to make the world we live in a more kind and healthy place. Let's do it—by maximizing the benefits to ourselves, to others, and to society, which can flourish as a result of applying the tools which allow us to think and act in healthy ways."

—Dr. Debbie Joffe Ellis, Psychologist; Author; Presenter

". . . I am sure that, if the 30-day plan outlined in Dr. Linda Elder and Dr. Richard Paul's book is followed consistently, it truly will improve the thinking and the lives of its readers. The 30-day regimen starts with the chapter 'Discover Your Ignorance' and moves along through chapters such as 'Empathize with Others,' 'Clarify Your Thinking,' 'Be Reasonable,' and 'Ask Deep Questions.' It is clearly inspired by Socrates, by his example of following the classical injunction 'Know Thyself,' questioning the conventional wisdom of himself and his fellow Athenians. Moreover, it is important that this critical thinking regimen is not merely a matter of acquiring skills, but is a deeply ethical endeavor. That is made crystal clear in chapters such as 'Be Fair, Not Selfish' and (one of my favorites) 'Don't Be Righteous: Show Mercy.' This small, easily readable book contains wisdom hard won during the two authors' dedicated and decades-long efforts to develop and communicate their conception of critical thinking, a conception that has rightly been very influential."

—Dr. Frank Fair, Sam Houston State University, Managing Editor
of *INQUIRY: Critical Thinking Across the Disciplines*

"*30 Days* is a manifesto for approaching life and relationships assertively, for thinking clearly and fairly, and for uncovering your own biases and vulnerabilities to the persuasive tactics of others. Stop being an underdog or a domineering top dog and read *30 Days*! *30 Days* is an excellent text for new graduate students to introduce them to the kind of logic and critical thinking that underlies scholarly thinking. A hands-on approach to helping anyone who wants to see the world around them more fairly and clearly."

—Dr. Karen E. Dill, Author of *How Fantasy Becomes Reality*

"A comprehensive and effective blueprint for getting one's thoughts on straight through the application of a proven intellectual concept to the practicalities of daily living. A critical thinking classic."

—George Hanford, President Emeritus, The College Board

"There is much to gain from reading books written by Dr. Linda Elder and Dr. Richard Paul. This book carries on their tradition of elevating our thinking into the stratosphere while keeping our feet planted firmly on practical ground. The turbulent, globalized twenty-first century world presents us with enormously complex and serious problems as well as unprecedented opportunities. If we are to survive and thrive in this environment, we need to employ much better thinking than we have in the past. Fortunately, this book is a high-quality toolkit containing sophisticated, powerful, creative and critical thinking tools. It's also fortunate that the authors provide easy-to-follow, jargon-free instructions for the use of these tools."

—Dr. Don Ambrose, Editor, *The Roeper Review*

"At a time when many Americans are faced with the need to make decisions on complex issues comes a book that offers a useful guide on how this can be accomplished. Using their conceptual scheme for critical thinking, Dr. Linda Elder and Dr. Richard Paul offer the reader a series of ideas, questions, and guidelines to help the reader develop clear thinking skills and to give the reader directions for living in a more rational and fairminded world. I have found that these clearly stated strategies accompanied by examples, the inclusion of well-developed visual graphics, and the in depth glossary of concepts make the book both practical and readable. The book is a necessary addition to anyone's personal library and a valuable guideline for understanding the need for critical thinking in one's daily life."

—Mel Manson, Professor of Sociology and Psychology, Endicott College

"Through their elegant and readable style, Dr. Linda Elder and Dr. Richard Paul, preeminent leaders in the Critical Thinking Community, show us how to objectively and honestly navigate the 'terrain' of critical thinking . . . to better employ the essential skills and art of critical thinking to enhance our self awareness, and our interactions and relations with family, colleagues, society. A truly valuable book!"

—Bill Messink, Oakton Community College

30 Days to Better Thinking and Better Living Through Critical Thinking

30 Days to Better Thinking and Better Living Through Critical Thinking

A Guide for Improving
Every Aspect of Your Life,
Revised and Expanded

Dr. Linda Elder and Dr. Richard Paul

Vice President, Publisher: Tim Moore
Associate Publisher and Director of Marketing: Amy Neidlinger
Executive Editor: Jim Boyd
Editorial Assistant: Pamela Boland
Development Editor: Russ Hall
Operations Specialist: Jodi Kemper
Assistant Marketing Manager: Megan Graue
Cover Designer: Alan Clements
Managing Editor: Kristy Hart
Project Editor: Jovana San Nicolas-Shirley
Copy Editor: Deadline Driven Publishing
Proofreader: Sarah Kearns
Senior Indexer: Cheryl Lenser
Compositor: Nonie Ratcliff
Manufacturing Buyer: Dan Uhrig

FT Press offers excellent discounts on this book when ordered in quantity for bulk purchases or special sales. For more information, please contact U.S. Corporate and Government Sales, 1-800-382-3419, corpsales@pearsontechgroup.com. For sales outside the U.S., please contact International Sales at international@pearsoned.com.

Company and product names mentioned herein are the trademarks or registered trademarks of their respective owners.

Printed in the United States of America

First Printing: September 2012

ISBN-10: 0-13-309256-9
ISBN-13: 978-0-13-309256-1

Pearson Education LTD.
Pearson Education Australia PTY, Limited.
Pearson Education Singapore, Pte. Ltd.
Pearson Education Asia, Ltd.
Pearson Education Canada, Ltd.
Pearson Educación de Mexico, S.A. de C.V.
Pearson Education—Japan
Pearson Education Malaysia, Pte. Ltd.

The Library of Congress cataloging-in-publication data is on file.

A special acknowledgment is due to Gerald Nosich—dedicated thinker, exemplary scholar, lifelong friend, and colleague.

Contents

    "But if my beliefs weren't true, I wouldn't believe them."

"The key to every man is his thought." —Emerson

"Of all knowledge, the wise and good seek most to know themselves." —Shakespeare

"Do you want to know the man against whom you have most reason to guard yourself? Your looking-glass will give you a very fair likeness of his face." —Whately

"The first step to knowledge is to know that we are ignorant." —Cecil

"The more you practice what you know, the more shall you know what to practice." —W. Jenkin

"Thinking is the hardest work there is, which is the probable reason why so few engage in it." —Henry Ford

"Thinking leads man to knowledge. He may see and hear, and read and learn whatever he pleases, and as much as he pleases; he will never know anything of it, except that which he has thought over, that which by thinking he has made the property of his own mind." —Pestalozzi

About the Authors

Dr. Linda Elder is an educational psychologist, executive director of the Center for Critical Thinking, and president of the Foundation for Critical Thinking. She is highly published and has a special interest in the relationship between cognition and effect, or thought and emotion. She has developed an original theory of the stages of critical-thinking development. She is a major keynote presenter at the *International Conference on Critical Thinking*, is highly sought after as a speaker, and is a recognized leader in critical thinking.

Dr. Richard Paul is founder of the Foundation for Critical Thinking and director of Research and Professional Development at the Center for Critical Thinking. He is an internationally recognized authority on critical thinking, with nine books and more than 200 articles on the subject. His views on critical thinking have been canvassed in the *New York Times*, *Education Week*, *The Chronicle of Higher Education*, *American Teacher*, *Reader's Digest*, *Educational Leadership*, *Newsweek*, and *U.S. News and World Report*.

The works of Linda Elder and Richard Paul have been translated into Spanish, French, German, Italian, Japanese, Polish, Chinese, Turkish, Greek, Thai, and Korean. The growing demand for translations into increasing numbers of languages testifies to the emerging international recognition of the importance of critical thinking in human life. It is a testament to the contributions of Paul and Elder to the growing field of critical thinking studies.

The **Foundation for Critical Thinking** seeks to promote essential change in society through the cultivation of fairminded critical thinking, thinking predisposed toward intellectual empathy, intellectual humility, intellectual perseverance, intellectual integrity, and intellectual responsibility. In a world of accelerating change, intensifying complexity, and increasing interdependence, critical thinking is now a requirement for economic and social survival. Contact the Foundation for Critical Thinking at www.criticalthinking.org.

Introduction

There is nothing we do as humans that does not involve thinking. Our thinking tells us what to believe, what to reject, what is important, what is unimportant, what is true, what is false, who are our friends, who our enemies are, how we should spend our time, what jobs we should pursue, where we should live, who we should marry, how we should parent. Everything we know, believe, want, fear, and hope for, our thinking tells us.

It follows, then, that the quality of our lives is primarily determined by the quality of our thinking. Our thinking has implications for how we go about doing literally everything we do.

The quality of your work is determined by the quality of your thinking as you reason through the problems you face as you work. The quality of your relationships is determined by the thinking you do in those relationships. Right now, as you read this book, the very sense you make of it comes from your thinking. Your ability to understand and internalize the ideas it contains will be determined by the quality of your thinking as you read it.

"Thinking is skilled work. It is not true that we are naturally endowed with the ability to think clearly and logically—without learning how, or without practicing... People with untrained minds should no more expect to think clearly and logically than those people who have never learned and never practiced can expect to find themselves good carpenters, golfers, bridge players, or pianists. Yet our world is full of people who apparently do suppose that thinking is entirely unskilled work; that thinking clearly and accurately is so easy and so 'natural' that 'anybody can think;' and that any person's thinking is quite as reliable as any other person's."
—A. E. Mander, Clear Thinking: Logic for Every Man, 1938

Therefore, learning to think critically is too important to leave to chance. Critical thinking is the disciplined art of ensuring that you use the best thinking you are capable of in any set of circumstances. Through developed critical capacities, you can take command of the thinking that commands you.

No matter what your circumstance or goals, no matter where you are or what problems you face, you are better off if you are in control of your thinking. As a professional, parent, citizen, lover, friend, shopper—in every realm and situation of your life—skilled thinking pays off. Poor thinking, in contrast, inevitably causes problems, wastes time and energy, and engenders frustration and pain.

Becoming a critical thinker requires that you learn to observe, monitor, analyze, assess, and reconstruct thinking of many sorts in many dimensions of human life. It requires building important habits of mind. It has implications for every act that takes place in your mind. It requires a special form of dedication and perseverance, honesty and integrity. It can be done only if taken seriously and pursued throughout a lifetime.

This book shows you how to use your mind to improve your mind. Each of the ideas in this book can help you take command of the mind that is controlling your thoughts, emotions, desires, and behavior.

Our hope is not in a miracle transformation, but in laying a foundation for your future intellectual and emotional growth. We are merely scratching the surface of deep and complex topics. We do not provide a quick fix, but rather places to begin. When you begin to take your intellectual growth seriously, you begin to see payoffs in every part of your life.

But first, you must wake up your mind. You must begin to understand your mind. You must begin to see when it causes you problems. You must begin to see when it causes others problems. You must learn how to trap it when it tries to hide from itself (using one of the many forms of self-deception at which it is naturally skilled). You must discover some of the trash and nonsense you have unknowingly taken in during years of passive absorption—to which all of us are subject. This book shows you how to begin.

The quality of your life is determined by the quality of your thinking.

Thinking gets us into trouble because we often:

- are unclear, muddled, or confused
- jump to conclusions
- fail to think through implications
- lose track of our goals
- are unrealistic
- focus on the trivial
- fail to notice contradictions
- accept inaccurate information
- ask vague questions
- give vague answers
- ask loaded questions
- ask irrelevant questions
- confuse questions of different types
- answer questions we are not competent to answer
- come to conclusions based on inaccurate or irrelevant information
- ignore information that does not support our view
- make inferences not justified by our experience
- distort data and present it inaccurately
- fail to notice our inferences
- fail to distinguish inferences from assumptions
- come to unreasonable conclusions
- fail to notice our assumptions
- make unjustified assumptions
- miss key ideas
- use irrelevant ideas
- form confused ideas
- form superficial concepts
- misuse words

- ignore relevant viewpoints
- cannot see issues from points of view other than our own
- confuse issues of different types
- are unaware of our prejudices
- think narrowly
- think imprecisely
- think illogically
- think one-sidedly
- think simplistically
- think hypocritically
- think superficially
- think sociocentrically
- think egocentrically
- think irrationally
- fail to reason well through problems
- make poor decisions
- are poor communicators
- lack insight into our ignorance

Improve Your Thinking, Improve Your Life

This book is about how to improve your thinking to improve your life. Why thinking? Why is thinking significant? Why try to improve your thinking?

The answer is simple: Only through thinking can you change whatever it is about your life that needs changing (even the parts you don't know need changing). Only through thinking can you take command of your future. Sound too simple? Read on.

Humans routinely (you might say almost constantly) think. For certain, thinking is the main thing we do. From the minute we wake up in the morning, we begin thinking. During all of our waking hours, we are thinking. We cannot escape our thinking, even if we want to.

Right now you are thinking about whether to take seriously what we are saying. Your thinking structures your feelings, shapes your desires, and guides your actions.[1] The way you think about parenting determines how you parent. The way you think about your financial situation determines the financial decisions you make. The way you think when you are at work determines how you function on the job.

The problem is that human thinking is often flawed. Many of our regrettable actions emerge from faulty reasoning. In fact, problems in thinking lead to more problems in life than perhaps any other single variable. They lead to conflict and war, pain and frustration, cruelty and suffering.

Yet, most people are content with their thinking. Because the development of thinking typically is not valued in human societies, people don't tend to trace the problems in their lives to problems in their thinking. Instead, they often live the whole of their lives without recognizing the leading role that thinking plays in it.

To improve your quality of life significantly, you must begin to take thinking seriously—to become a student, if you will, of thinking. You must begin to observe thinking, examine it, witness its power in action. You must begin to discipline your thinking through knowledge of thinking, and you should practice using that knowledge (of thinking) daily. You must begin to analyze your thinking, assess your thinking, and improve your thinking. You must engage in *critical* thinking.

This book explores some of the basic facts about thinking. Although the study of thinking and its relationship to emotions and desires are complex, most everyone can access its essential ideas. The trick is to use basic principles systematically to change your life for the better. In other words, the trick is to put critical thinking into action in your life. You can learn it. You can use it. This book provides some of the essential building blocks.

---

1. For an introduction to the relationships between thinking, feeling, and wanting, see *The Miniature Guide to the Human Mind* by Elder, L. and Paul, R. Dillon Beach: Foundation for Critical Thinking (2002).

Can Your Thinking Be Your Problem?

To begin to take thinking seriously, you must first recognize the inherently flawed nature of human thought in its "normal" state. Put another way, without active intervention, human thinking naturally develops problems. For example, humans are prejudiced. We stereotype one another. We are often hypocritical. We sometimes justify in our own minds policies and practices that result in stealing, killing, and torture. We often ignore important problems that we could, with determination and good thinking, solve—problems such as world hunger, poverty, and homelessness.

What is more, when we behave irrationally, our behavior usually seems reasonable to us. When challenged, the mind says (to itself), "Why are these people giving me a hard time? I'm just doing what makes sense. Any reasonable person would see that!" In short, we naturally think that our thinking is fully justified. As far as we can tell, we are only doing what is right and proper and reasonable. Any fleeting thoughts suggesting that we might be at fault typically are overcome by more powerful self-justifying thoughts: "I don't mean any harm. I'm just! I'm fair! It's the others who are wrong!"

It is important to recognize this self-justifying nature of the human mind as its *natural state*. In other words, humans don't have to learn self-justifying, self-serving, self-deceptive thinking, and behavior. These patterns are innate in every one of us. How does self-deception work in the mind? In other words, how can it be that we can see ourselves as right even when readily available evidence proves us wrong? One powerful reason is the mind's *native* ability to represent unreasonable thoughts as perfectly reasonable. Indeed, this is perhaps the most significant reason that humans fail to recognize their own irrationality.

For example, consider the female supervisor who, after interviewing both male and female applicants, always hires women.[2] This supervisor considers herself unbiased and objective. When asked

---

2. Consider also the male supervisor who hires only men.

why she hires only female employees, she most likely would give what appear to be logical reasons to support her decisions—facts, for example, about the applicants' work experiences, skills, and so on. In supporting her hiring decisions, she would see herself as even-handed, as simply trying to hire the best employees for the job. She might at some level recognize that she hires only women, but justify it by arguing that women are somehow naturally better in the jobs she oversees. Indeed, the only way she can feel justified *in her own mind* is to see herself as behaving objectively. The material point is that biased thinking appears to the mind as dispassionate, unprejudiced, impartial thinking. We don't see ourselves as wrong. Rather, we see ourselves as right, as doing what is most reasonable in the situation, even when we are dead wrong.

Consider the police officer who often uses excessive force during arrests. This officer likely sees himself as giving criminals what they deserve, getting them off the streets so they can't harm innocent people. He couldn't act in this way if he recognized the role that prejudice and the desire for power were playing in his thinking, if he could see that he was irrationally using unnecessary power and force—over others who were unable to defend themselves. In his own mind, he is professional and just. However cruel he may be, he doesn't see himself as such. Such is the power of self-deception.

Welcome to human nature. We are all, to varying degrees, prejudiced. We all stereotype and deceive ourselves. We see ourselves as possessing *the truth*. Yet we all fall prey to human egocentricity—although not to the same degree. None of us will ever be a perfect thinker, but we can all be *better* thinkers.

To develop as a thinker, you need to work daily to bring what is unconscious in your thinking to the level of consciousness. You need to discover the problems that exist in your thinking and face them. Only then can you make significant improvements in your thinking and your life. Inherent in human nature is the capacity to rise above your native egocentric patterns of thought. You can use your mind to educate your mind. You can use your thinking to change your thinking. You can "remake" or "transform" yourself. It is this side of your nature we hope to stimulate as you work through and internalize the ideas in this book.

A How-To List for Dysfunctional Living

One of the ways you can enhance the power of your mind is by learning to create contrasts and oppositions that make clear precisely what you need to avoid. In other words, by making poor habits of thought more and more explicit, you get better and better at avoiding them.

We now illustrate this strategy by constructing a set of rules that no reasonable person would knowingly follow. By illuminating dysfunctional, even pathological, ways of thinking, it becomes obvious how easy it is to fall prey to them without recognizing yourself doing so.

Consider the following, and ask yourself how many of these dysfunctional ways of thinking you engage in:

1. **Surround yourself with people who think like you.** Then no one will criticize you.

2. **Don't question your relationships.** You then can avoid dealing with problems within them.

3. **If critiqued by a friend or lover, look sad and dejected** and say, "I thought you were my friend!" or "I thought you loved me!"

4. **When you do something unreasonable, always be ready with an excuse.** Then you won't have to take responsibility. If you can't think of an excuse, look sorry and say, "I can't help how I am!"

5. **Focus on the negative side of life.** Then you can make yourself miserable and blame it on others.

6. **Blame others for your mistakes.** Then you won't have to feel responsible for your mistakes nor will you have to do anything about them.

7. **Verbally attack those who criticize you.** Then you don't have to bother listening to what they say.

8. **Go along with the groups you are in.** Then you won't have to figure out anything for yourself.

9. **Act out when you don't get what you want.** If questioned, look indignant and say, "I'm just an emotional person. At least I don't keep my feelings bottled up!"

10. **Focus on getting what you want.** If questioned, say, "If I don't look out for number one, who will?"

This list would be almost laughable if these irrational ways of thinking didn't lead to problems in life. But they do. And often. Only when you are faced with the absurdity of dysfunctional or even pathological thinking and can see it at work in your life do you have a chance to alter it. The strategies outlined in this book presuppose your willingness to do so.

Take Your Thinking Seriously

Our goal is to help you begin to think *critically* about your thinking, to think about the ways in which your thinking might be causing problems for you or others. As you work through the ideas in this book, simple ideas intelligently applied, you will begin to improve the habits of your mind. You will become aware of your thinking. When you do, you will assess it. When you assess it, you will improve it.

Think of yourself as your own private investigator, probing the workings of your mind to figure out what is going on inside its mental walls. Once you sort out some of the patterns that dominate your thinking, you can take your thinking to the next level; you can target those patterns for improvement. You can build on your strengths. You can determine what to retain in your thinking and what to throw out, which of your beliefs are sensible and which are senseless, which are causing problems, which are bringing richness to your life, which are entrapping or limiting you, and which are freeing or liberating you.

No Intellectual Pain, No Intellectual Gain

Although most people readily agree that a *no pain, no gain* attitude is necessary for physical fitness, those same people often give up at the first sign of mental discomfort when working on their minds. If you are unwilling to persevere through intellectual pain, you simply will not develop as a thinker. Without some stress, the condition of the mind, like the body, will not improve. Like it or not, one undeniable fact is *no intellectual pain, no intellectual gain*.

So expect some mental stress, discomfort, and pain as you proceed through this book. When it comes, face it and work through it. Realize that the most important ideas humans need to learn are often among the most difficult for the mind to understand and accept (like the fact that we are all naturally egocentric). Recognize that the mind, by nature, resists change—especially change that would force it to see itself in an unfavorable light. So, as you begin to internalize the ideas in this book and feel frustrated, uncomfortable, or discouraged, keep pushing forward. Celebrate the fact that you are growing, rather than standing still, like most people. Realize that the reward is in the improved quality of your life that will occur in the long run. You must stretch and work the mind if you want it to become flexible and powerful, and if you want it to do the work, you need it to do in the many dimensions of your life.

The Concepts, Principles, and Tools of Critical Thinking

To this point, we have argued that thinking about thinking in a disciplined way is largely ignored in human societies, and that it needs to be at the center of how we live every day. When we realize there are many problems in human thought and we want to explicitly target these problems, we can intervene in thought. But we need tools for doing this. And these tools need to emerge from a rich, substantive approach to the mind, not one that is simplistic or superficial. For instance, we need a concept that helps us deal with our intrinsic

selfish and self-validating tendencies. We need a rich concept of critical thought that helps us deal with the forces within us that lead us to
seek uncritical approval from others. We need a concept that helps
us live more reasonably in all parts of our lives, as well as one that
helps us adhere to reasonable standards for thought—standards like
clarity, accuracy, relevance, depth, breadth, logicalness, and fairness.
We need a concept of critical thinking that helps us take our thinking apart and examine each part for quality. We need a concept that
guides us to fairminded, critical societies.

> As you work through the book, see if you can figure out how
> each day's idea is related to one or more critical thinking con-
> cepts in this section.

In this section, we briefly introduce a conception of critical thinking that has emerged through our work in the last three decades. To
help make the ideas embedded in critical thinking intuitive, we present them primarily in graphic form.[3] Each of the "30-days" ideas in
this book is intimately connected with this concept. Some are connected to the *analysis of thought*, some to the *assessment of thought*,
some to the development of *intellectual virtues*. Others focus on the
barriers to critical thought (or pathologies in human thought), which
we can place under the rough umbrellas of *egocentric* and *sociocentric* thought. And still others are implications or contextualizations of
critical thought.

There is no perfect way to learn critical thinking, no definite order
to it. Instead, there are many powerful ideas in critical thinking, any
one of which, if deeply internalized can profoundly change the way
you live. Consider, for instance, intellectual empathy, which entails
the developed propensity to think within other viewpoints, to think

---

3. For a more in-depth understanding of critical thinking, read *Critical Thinking:
   Tools for Taking Charge of Your Professional and Personal Life* by Richard Paul
   and Linda Elder (2002). Upper Saddle River, NJ: Pearson Prentice Hall.

the thoughts and feel the emotions of others in order to appreciate and understand their perspectives. If everyone in the world were to take this idea seriously, the pain and suffering caused by humans would be greatly reduced. For instance, people would, almost naturally, imagine what it would be like to experience the feelings of those they were controlling, dominating, oppressing, manipulating, or otherwise mistreating. People would almost literally feel one another's pain. By implication, they would come to more highly value living together peacefully and respectfully. We would move closer to the realization of fairminded, critical societies. Of course, keep in mind that this way of putting the point is somewhat oversimplified because all the concepts in critical thinking are interconnected. To develop deep and transformative understanding of any one idea in critical thinking is to develop deep and transformative understanding of other essential ideas in critical thinking. For instance, to cultivate within ourselves intellectual empathy, we must also cultivate intellectual humility, the tendency to uncover one's own ignorance, to separate what we know from what we don't know. We cannot effectively think within alternate viewpoints (intellectual empathy) if we are not inclined to identify our knowledge and our ignorance within these viewpoints (intellectual humility).

In short, the concepts and principles of critical thinking should ultimately be understood in connection with one another, hence the impetus for this section—to help you see some of the important connections among all the ideas in this book. People throughout the world now embrace a rich, substantive, integrated concept of critical thinking (not nearly enough, though). We welcome you to this complex of ideas.

Why Critical Thinking?

The Problem:

Everyone thinks; it is our nature to do so. But much of our thinking, left to itself, is biased, distorted, partial, uninformed, or down-right prejudiced. Yet the quality of our life and that of what we produce, make, or build depends precisely on the quality of our thought. Shoddy thinking is costly, both in money and in quality of life. Excellence in thought, however, must be systematically cultivated.

A Definition:

Critical thinking, in a rich sense of the term, is self-guided disciplined thought that attempts to reason at the highest level of quality in a fairminded way. People who think critically consistently attempt to live rationally, reasonably, and with empathy. They are keenly aware of the inherently flawed nature of human thinking when left unchecked. They strive to diminish the power of their egocentric and sociocentric tendencies. They use the intellectual tools that critical thinking offers–concepts and principles that enable them to analyze, assess, and improve thinking. They realize that no matter how skilled they are as thinkers, at times they will fall prey to mistakes in reasoning, to irrationality, prejudices, biases, distortions, uncritically accepted social rules and taboos, selfish interest, and vested interest. They avoid thinking simplistically about complicated issues and strive to appropriately consider the rights and needs of relevant others. They embody the Socratic principle: The unexamined life is not worth living. They are concerned with their own intellectual development as well as the cultivation of fairminded critical societies.

The Result:

A well-cultivated critical thinker:

- Raises vital questions and problems, formulating them clearly and precisely;
- Gathers and assesses relevant information, using abstract ideas to interpret it effectively
- Comes to well-reasoned conclusions and solutions, testing them against relevant criteria and standards
- Thinks openmindedly within alternative systems of thought, recognizing and assessing, as need be, their assumptions, implications, and practical consequences and
- Communicates effectively with others in figuring out solutions to complex problems

Critical thinking is, in short, self-directed, self-disciplined, self-monitored, and self-corrective thinking. It requires rigorous standards of excellence and mindful command of their use. It entails effective communication and problem solving abilities and a commitment to overcoming our native egocentrism and sociocentrism.

The Figuring Mind

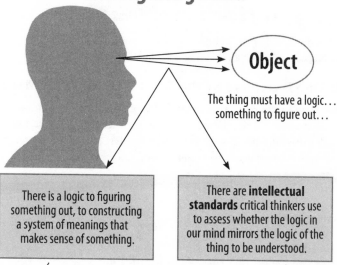

Object

The thing must have a logic...
something to figure out...

There is a logic to figuring something out, to constructing a system of meanings that makes sense of something.

There are **intellectual standards** critical thinkers use to assess whether the logic in our mind mirrors the logic of the thing to be understood.

The Elements of Thought reveal the logic:

1	An object to be figured out ⟶	Some data or information, some experience of it (the **Empirical Dimension**)
2	Some reason for wanting to figure it out ⟶	Our **Purpose** or **Goal**
3	Some question or problem we want solved ⟶	Our **Question at Issue**
4	Some initial sense of the object (whatever we take for granted) ⟶	Our **Assumptions**
5	Some ideas by which we are making sense of the object ⟶	The **Conceptual Dimension**
6	Some drawing of conclusions about the object ⟶	Our **Inferences** or interpretations
7	What follows from our interpretation of the object ⟶	The **Implications** and **Consequences**
8	Some viewpoint from which we conceptualize the object ⟶	Our **Point of View** or **Frame of Reference**

Intellectual Standards include:

Clarity

Precision

Relevance

Accuracy

Depth

Breadth

Logic

Fairness

Analyze Your Thinking (Focusing on the Elements of Reasoning)

If we want to think well, we must understand at least the rudiments of thought, the most basic structures out of which all thinking is made. We must learn how to take thinking apart.

All Thinking Is Defined by the Eight Elements That Make It Up

Eight basic structures are present in all thinking: Whenever we think, we think for a purpose within a point of view based on assumptions leading to implications and consequences. We use concepts, ideas, and theories to interpret data, facts, and experiences in order to answer questions, solve problems, and resolve issues.

Thinking, then:

- Generates purposes

- Raises questions

- Uses information

- Utilizes concepts

- Makes inferences

- Makes assumptions

- Generates implications

- Embodies a point of view

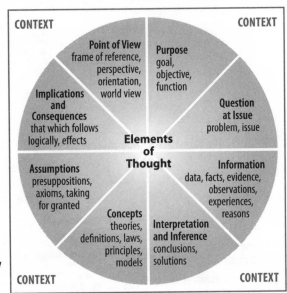

Each of these structures has implications for the others. If you change your purpose or agenda, you change your questions and problems. If you change your questions and problems, you are forced to seek new information and data. If you collect new information and data…

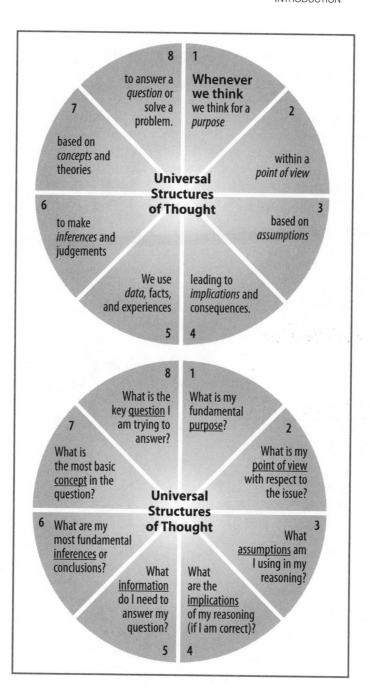

8 to answer a *question* or solve a problem.

1 **Whenever we think** we think for a *purpose*

2 within a *point of view*

3 based on *assumptions*

4 leading to *implications* and consequences.

5 We use *data,* facts, and experiences

6 to make *inferences* and judgements

7 based on *concepts* and theories

Universal Structures of Thought

---

8 What is the key question I am trying to answer?

1 What is my fundamental purpose?

2 What is my point of view with respect to the issue?

3 What assumptions am I using in my reasoning?

4 What are the implications of my reasoning (if I am correct)?

5 What information do I need to answer my question?

6 What are my most fundamental inferences or conclusions?

7 What is the most basic concept in the question?

Universal Structures of Thought

Assess Your Thinking
(Using Reasonable Standards)

Reasonable people judge reasoning by intellectual standards. When you internalize these standards and explicitly use them in your thinking, your thinking becomes more clear, more accurate, more precise, more relevant, deeper, broader, and more fair. You should note that we focus here on a selection of standards. Among others are credibility, sufficiency, reliability, and practicality. Some questions that employ these standards are listed on the following page.

Clarity: understandable, the meaning can be grasped

Accuracy: free from errors or distortions, true

Precision: exact to the necessary level of detail

Relevance: relating to the matter at hand

Depth: containing complexities and multiple interrelationships

Breadth: encompassing multiple viewpoints

Logic: the parts make sense together, no contradictions

Significance: focusing on the important, not trivial

Fairness: justifiable, not self-serving or one-sided

Clarity
Could you elaborate further?
Could you give me an example?
Could you illustrate what you mean?

Accuracy
How could we check on that?
How could we find out if that is true?
How could we verify or test that?

Precision
Could you be more specific?
Could you give me more details?
Could you be more exact?

Relevance
How does that relate to the problem?
How does that bear on the question?
How does that help us with the issue?

Depth
What factors make this a difficult problem?
What are some of the complexities of this question?
What are some of the difficulties we need to deal with?

Breadth
Do we need to look at this from another perspective?
Do we need to consider another point of view?
Do we need to look at this in other ways?

Logic
Does all this make sense together?
Does your first paragraph fit in with your last?
Does what you say follow from the evidence?

Significance
Is this the most important problem to consider?
Is this the central idea to focus on?
Which of these facts are most important?

Fairness
Do I have any vested interest in this issue?
Am I sympathetically representing the viewpoints of others?

Systematically Apply Intellectual Standards to the Elements of Reasoning to Develop Intellectual Traits

THE STANDARDS

Clarity	Precision
Accuracy	Significance
Relevance	Completeness
Logicalness	Fairness
Breadth	Depth

Must be applied to

THE ELEMENTS

Purposes	Inferences
Questions	Concepts
Points of View	Implications
Information	Assumptions

As we learn to develop

INTELLECTUAL TRAITS

Intellectual Humility	Intellectual Perseverance
Intellectual Autonomy	Confidence in Reason
Intellectual Integrity	Intellectual Empathy
Intellectual Courage	Fairmindedness

Pursue the Constellation of Intellectual Traits

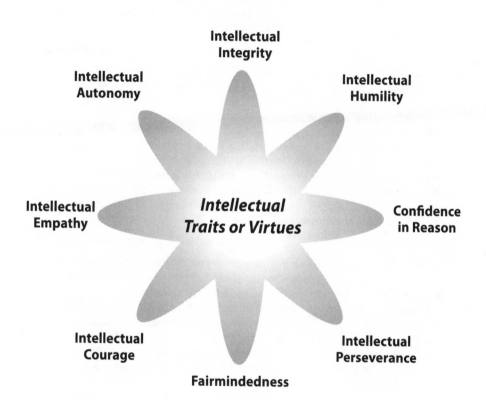

Intellectual
Integrity

Intellectual
Autonomy

Intellectual
Humility

Intellectual
Empathy

*Intellectual
Traits or Virtues*

Confidence
in Reason

Intellectual
Courage

Intellectual
Perseverance

Fairmindedness

Intellectual Humility   Versus Intellectual Arrogance

Having a consciousness of the limits of one's knowledge, including a sensitivity to circumstances in which one's native egocentrism is likely to function self-deceptively; sensitivity to bias, prejudice, and limitations of one's viewpoint. Intellectual humility depends on recognizing that one should not claim more than one actually knows. It does not imply spinelessness or submissiveness. It implies the lack of intellectual pretentiousness, boastfulness, or conceit, combined with insight into the logical foundations, or lack of such foundations, of one's beliefs.

Intellectual Courage   Versus Intellectual Cowardice

Having a consciousness of the need to face and fairly address ideas, beliefs, or viewpoints toward which we have strong negative emotions and to which we have not given a serious hearing. This courage is connected with the recognition that ideas considered dangerous or absurd are sometimes rationally justified (in whole or in part) and that conclusions and beliefs inculcated in us are sometimes false or misleading. To determine for ourselves which is which, we must not passively and uncritically "accept" what we have "learned." Intellectual courage comes into play here, because inevitably we will come to see some truth in some ideas considered dangerous and absurd, and distortion or falsity in some ideas strongly held in our social group. We need courage to be true to our own thinking in such circumstances. The penalties for nonconformity can be severe.

Intellectual Empathy   Versus Intellectual Narrow-mindedness

Having a consciousness of the need to imaginatively put oneself in the place of others in order to genuinely understand them, which requires the consciousness of our egocentric tendency to identify truth with our immediate perceptions of long-standing thought or belief. This trait correlates with the ability to reconstruct accurately the viewpoints and reasoning of others and to reason from premises, assumptions, and ideas other than our own. This trait also correlates with the willingness to remember occasions when we were wrong in the past despite an intense conviction that we were right, and with the ability to imagine our being similarly deceived in a case-at-hand.

Intellectual Autonomy   Versus Intellectual Conformity

Having rational control of one's beliefs, values, and inferences. The ideal of critical thinking is to learn to think for oneself, to gain command over one's thought processes. It entails a commitment to analyzing and evaluating beliefs on the basis of reason and evidence, to question when it is rational to question, to believe when it is rational to believe, and to conform when it is rational to conform.

Intellectual Integrity   Versus Intellectual Hypocrisy

Recognition of the need to be true to one's own thinking; to be consistent in the intellectual standards one applies; to hold one's self to the same rigorous standards of evidence and proof to which one holds one's antagonists; to practice what one advocates for others; and to honestly admit discrepancies and inconsistencies in one's own thought and action.

Intellectual Perseverance   Versus Intellectual Laziness

Having a consciousness of the need to use intellectual insights and truths in spite of difficulties, obstacles, and frustrations; firm adherence to rational principles despite the irrational opposition of others; a sense of the need to struggle with confusion and unsettled questions over an extended period of time to achieve deeper understanding or insight.

Confidence In Reason   Versus Distrust of Reason and Evidence

Confidence that, in the long run, one's own higher interests and those of humankind at large will be best served by giving the freest play to reason, by encouraging people to come to their own conclusions by developing their own rational faculties; faith that, with proper encouragement and cultivation, people can learn to think for themselves, to form rational viewpoints, draw reasonable conclusions, think coherently and logically, persuade each other by reason and become reasonable persons, despite the deep-seated obstacles in the native character of the human mind and in society as we know it.

Fairmindedness   Versus Intellectual Unfairness

Having a consciousness of the need to treat all viewpoints alike, without reference to one's own feelings or vested interests, or the feelings or vested interests of one's friends, community, or nation; implies adherence to intellectual standards without reference to one's own advantage or the advantage of one's group.

Understand the Mind's Three Distinctive Functions

The mind has three basic functions: thinking, feeling, and wanting.

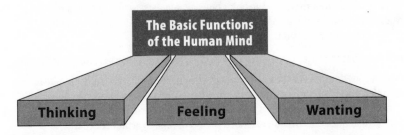

- Thinking is the part of the mind that figures things out. It makes sense of life's events. It creates the ideas through which we define situations, relationships, and problems. It continually tells us: This is what is going on. This is what is happening. Notice this and that.

- Feelings* are created by thinking—evaluating whether the events of our lives are positive or negative. Feelings continually tell us: "This is how I should feel about what is happening in my life. I'm doing really well." Or, alternatively, "Things aren't going well for me."

- Our desires allocate energy to action, in keeping with what we define as desirable and possible. It continually tells us: "This is worth getting. Go for it!" Or, conversely, "This is not worth getting. Don't bother."

* When we speak of feelings, we are not referring to emotions caused by dysfunctional biological processes such as problems in brain chemistry. When emotions are caused by imbalances in brain chemistry that people cannot control themselves, clinical help may be needed. When we speak of feelings, we are also not referring to bodily sensations, though feelings often accompany bodily sensations. For instance, being "cold" might cause you to feel irritable. Recognizing the feeling of irritability might lead you to do something about being cold, like putting on a jacket. Finally, though the terms "feelings" and "emotions" might be used in some cases to refer to different phenomena, we use these terms interchangeably in this book.

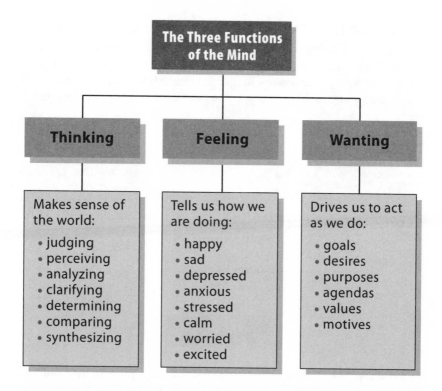

Essential Idea: Our mind is continually communicating three kinds of things to us:

- What is going on in life
- Feelings (positive or negative) about those events
- Things to pursue, where to put our energy (in light of 1 and 2)

Recognize Thinking as the Key to Feelings and Desires

Though thoughts, feelings, and desires play equally important roles in the mind, continually influencing and being influenced by one another, thinking is the key to command of feelings and desires. To change a feeling is to change the thinking that leads to the feeling. To change a desire is to change the thinking that underlies the desire.

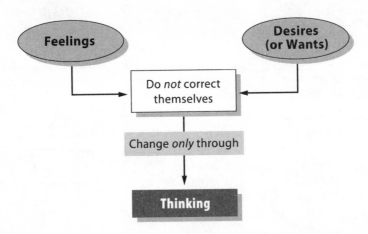

If I feel angry because my child is behaving disrespectfully toward me, I can't simply replace anger with satisfaction, for example. To change the anger to a more positive emotion, I must change the thinking I am doing in the situation. Perhaps I need to think about how to teach my child to behave respectfully toward me, and then behave in accordance with that new thinking. Perhaps I need to think about the influences in my child's life that might be causing the rude behavior and then try to eliminate those influences. In other words, I get control of my emotional state through my thinking.

Similarly, we can't change a desire without changing the thinking that causes the desire. Suppose, for example, two people, Jan and John, have been in a romantic relationship but John has broken off the relationship. Yet Jan still wants to be in the relationship. Suppose that her desire comes from thinking (that may be unconscious) that she needs to be in the relationship to be emotionally stable, that she won't be able to function without John. Clearly this thinking is the problem. Jan must therefore change her thinking so she no longer wants a relationship with John. In other words, until she thinks that she does not need John to be okay, that she can function satisfactorily without him, that she doesn't need to be in a relationship with a person who doesn't want to be with her, she will want to be in the relationship with John. In short, unless her thinking changes, her desire won't change. She must defeat the thinking that is defeating her.

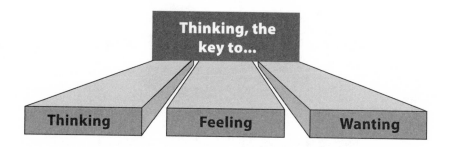

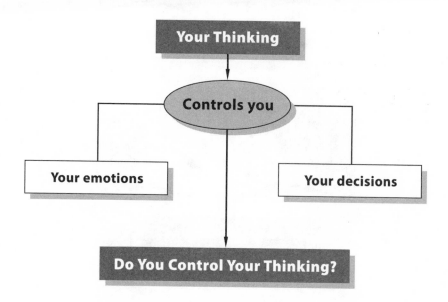

Distinguish Rational from Egocentric and Sociocentric Thoughts

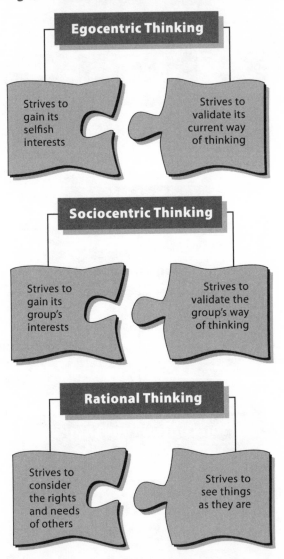

Essential Idea: It is important to distinguish egocentric and sociocentric motives from rational motives.

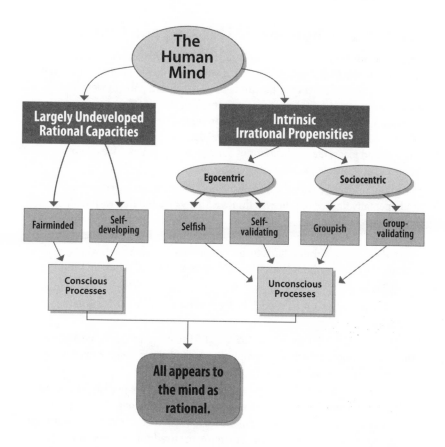

Essential Idea: All humans are innately egocentric and sociocentric. Humans also have (largely undeveloped) rational capacities. Humans begin life as primarily egocentric creatures. Over time, infantile egocentric self-centered thinking merges with sociocentric group-centered thinking. All humans regularly engage in both forms of irrational thought. The extent to which any of us is egocentric or sociocentric is a matter of degree and can change significantly in various situations or contexts. While egocentric and sociocentric propensities are naturally occurring phenomena, rational capacities must be largely developed. It is through the development of rational capacities that we combat irrational tendencies and cultivate critical societies.

Understand Egocentric Thinking as a Problem

Egocentric thinking results from the unfortunate fact that humans do not naturally consider the rights and needs of others. We do not naturally appreciate the point of view of others nor the limitations in our own point of view. We become explicitly aware of our egocentric thinking only if trained to do so. We do not naturally recognize our egocentric assumptions, the egocentric way we use information, the egocentric way we interpret data, the source of our egocentric concepts and ideas, the implications of our egocentric thought. We do not naturally recognize our self-serving perspective.

As humans we live with the unrealistic but confident sense that we have fundamentally figured out the way things actually are, and that we have done this objectively. We naturally believe in our intuitive perceptions—however inaccurate. Instead of using intellectual standards in thinking, we often use self-centered psychological standards to determine what to believe and what to reject. Here are the most commonly used psychological standards in human thinking.

"IT'S TRUE BECAUSE I BELIEVE IT." Innate egocentrism: I assume that what I believe is true, even though I have never questioned the basis for many of my beliefs.

"IT'S TRUE BECAUSE WE BELIEVE IT." Innate sociocentrism: I assume that the dominant beliefs of the groups to which I belong are true, even though I have never questioned the basis for those beliefs.

"IT'S TRUE BECAUSE I WANT TO BELIEVE IT." Innate wish fulfillment: I believe in whatever puts me (or the groups to which I belong) in a positive light. I believe what "feels good," what does not require me to change my thinking in any significant way, what does not require me to admit I have been wrong.

"IT'S TRUE BECAUSE I HAVE ALWAYS BELIEVED IT." Innate self-validation: I have a strong desire to maintain beliefs that I have long held, even though I have not seriously considered the extent to which those beliefs are justified by the evidence.

"IT'S TRUE BECAUSE IT IS IN MY SELFISH INTEREST TO BELIEVE IT." Innate selfishness: I believe whatever justifies my getting more power, money, or personal advantage even though these beliefs are not grounded in sound reasoning or evidence.

Distinguish Egocentric Domination
from Egocentric Submission

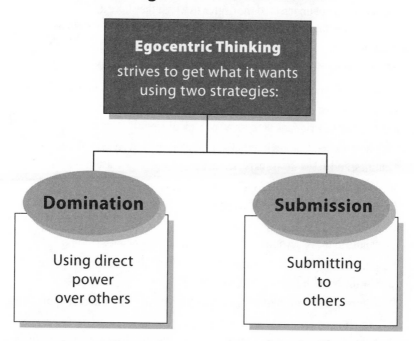

Egocentric Thinking

strives to get what it wants
using two strategies:

Domination

Using direct
power
over others

Submission

Submitting
to
others

Essential Idea: Two irrational ways to gain and use power are given in two distinct forms of egocentric strategy:

1) The art of dominating others (a direct means to getting what one wants).

2) The art of submitting to others (an indirect means to getting what one wants).

Insofar as we are thinking egocentrically, we seek to satisfy our egocentric desires either directly or indirectly, by exercising power and control over others, or by submitting to those who can act to serve our interest. To put it crudely, egocentric behavior either bullies or grovels. It either threatens those weaker or subordinates itself to those more powerful, or oscillates between them in subtle maneuvers and schemes.

Understand Sociocentric Thinking as a Problem

Most people do not understand the degree to which they have uncritically internalized the dominant prejudices of their society or culture. Sociologists and anthropologists identify this as the state of being "culture bound." This phenomenon is caused by sociocentric thinking, which includes:

- The uncritical tendency to place one's culture, nation, and religion above all others.
- The uncritical tendency to select self-serving positive descriptions of ourselves and negative descriptions of those who think differently from us.
- The uncritical tendency to internalize group norms and beliefs, take on group identities, and act as we are expected to act—without the least sense that what we are doing might reasonably be questioned.
- The tendency to blindly conform to group restrictions (many of which are arbitrary or coercive).
- The failure to think beyond the traditional prejudices of one's culture.
- The failure to study and internalize the insights of other cultures (improving thereby the breadth and depth of one's thinking).
- The failure to distinguish universal ethics from relativistic cultural requirements and taboos.
- The failure to realize that mass media in every culture shapes the news from the point of view of that culture.
- The failure to think historically and anthropologically (and hence, to be trapped in current ways of thinking).
- The failure to see sociocentric thinking as a significant impediment to intellectual development.

Sociocentric thinking is a hallmark of an uncritical society. It can be diminished only when replaced by cross-cultural, fairminded thinking—critical thinking in the strong sense.

A Substantive Approach
to Critical Thinking Targets

The analysis of thought
(focused on the elements of reasoning)

The assessment of thought
(using intellectual standards)

The
cultivation of
intellectual traits

With concern for the barriers to criticality

egocentricity

sociocentricity

The Thirty-Day Plan

This book introduces 30 fundamental ideas about thinking that form the basis of your 30-day plan. We include some of the important ideas we believe people need to grasp if they are to take command of their thinking and their lives. There is nothing magical about the number 30 rather than, say, 24, 32, or 35. And there are always new and important ideas to be learned—ideas that, when internalized and applied, help us think and live better. The development of thinking, you will discover, is an ongoing dynamic process.

We provide the ideas in a 30-day format so you can get an initial feel for the whole. You also can get an overview and begin to experience the power of ideas aimed at the improvement of thought. As you move through the 30 days, you will realize you cannot *internalize* any of these ideas in one day. Nevertheless, you can *begin* to bring important and powerful ideas into your thinking and *begin* to practice using them as agents for mental (intellectual) change.

On the first day, you focus on just one idea. On the second day, you focus on a second idea in light of the first. On the third day, you focus on the third idea in light of the second and the first. Each day, the tapestry becomes richer. Each day, you add a new and powerful idea to your thinking. As you proceed, you will always have a central focus, but your central focus is enriched through the background logic of, and interaction with, other powerful ideas.

As you move from day to day, you should try to integrate previously learned ideas with new ones. Having powerful ideas interact with other powerful ideas is a key to success. Long-term success largely depends on how you proceed after you complete the 30 days. Do you keep and use the ideas? Do you forget them? Do you pursue additional important ideas that connect with these ideas? Do you go back to the way you were before you read this book? Do you move forward? These are the kinds of questions you must ask, and revisit again and again, if you want to continue developing as a free and independent thinker.

Use the daily action plans and progress notes in the back of this section to plan and assess your progress as you move through each day.

Keep daily notes to deeply internalize each day's idea. See pages 42-43 for a suggested format.

Expanding to a 30-Week Plan

One way to proceed after you work through the 30-day plan is to advance to a 30-week plan, focusing on one idea per week, rather than one idea per day. In this advanced phase, as you move forward from week to week, you will find the power of each idea being intensified by new interactions with previous ideas. You will begin to see the interrelationships between and among the ideas. Whenever you take important ideas seriously and begin working them into your thinking, you will begin to see that every important idea has many connections to other important ideas. Powerful ideas are powerful *in light of* their important connections.

So we suggest a 30-day sprint to get the ideas flowing. Then a follow-up, longer-term, second run to deepen and further interconnect the ideas and begin to permanently internalize them.

The 30-week plan helps you build good habits of thought as each new idea adds to and connects with ideas learned in previous weeks. For example, following the 30-week plan, you will:

- Concentrate on *uncovering the extent of your ignorance* in the first week.

- Look out for *hypocrisy* in the second week—look for it in yourself and others (as a matter of secondary emphasis, though, you should still look for opportunities to *uncover deficiencies in your thinking*).

- Focus on *empathizing with others* whenever and however you can in the third week (while also *uncovering ignorance* in your thinking and looking out for hypocrisy).

> Keep weekly notes to deeply internalize the ideas running through this book. See pages 44-45 for a suggested format.

When you have internalized the first three ideas in this book, you will realize that endless problems in thinking occur precisely because people often fail to empathize, to differentiate what they know from what they do not know (but assume they know), and to seek out hypocrisy (in themselves and others). Moreover, you should recognize that our propensity to empathize with others increases as we become less intellectually arrogant, less sure that what we think is true must always be true, and, as we become more aware of hypocrisy in our own thinking and more aware of how often we expect more from others than we expect from ourselves.

And so it goes from week to week. Every week you focus on a new and important idea. As you add a new idea, you connect it with ideas already learned.

Periodically you should review all the ideas you have covered and determine whether you need to refresh in your mind one or more of the ideas previously covered. The more often you crisscross the terrain of important and powerful ideas, the more deeply they become embedded in your thinking and the more likely you are to use them in your life.

What is most important, as you expand to a weekly plan, is that at any given time you have a specific focus and that this focus is of sufficient duration. Feel free to move around within the ideas—there is no magic order.

You Will Reach a Payoff Point

When you have worked through the 30 ideas as recommended in this book, applying them on a daily or weekly basis, you should begin to experience payoffs in your life. You should find that

- You are better at communicating your ideas and understanding others.

- You are better at sticking to issues and solving problems.
- You pursue more rational goals and can better reach them.
- You are better at asking productive questions.
- You are less selfish.
- You have more control over your emotions.
- You have more control over your desires and behavior.
- You can better understand the viewpoints of others.
- You are more reasonable.
- You are less controlling.
- You are less submissive, less easily intimidated.
- You no longer worry about things you can't do anything about.
- You are less likely to irrationally blame others.
- You think through implications before acting.
- You are more comfortable admitting when you are wrong, and you seek to correct your faulty beliefs.
- You work to become a person of integrity, living up to a consistent, rational self-image, and you surround yourself with people of integrity.
- You begin to question social conventions and taboos.
- You begin to question what you read, hear, and see in the news media.
- You are less easily manipulated by smooth-talking, self-interested politicians.
- You are more aware of the ways in which you use words and how your understanding of reality is influenced by your word choice.
- You are able to identify the assumptions that lead to your inferences and conclusions (so you can check your assumptions for justifiability).
- You realize that all people see themselves as critical thinkers (and therefore not in need of improvement), which is one of the great barriers to the cultivation of critical societies.

- You are less likely to use words in ways that are not justified given educated usage.

- You are more concerned with the rights and needs of all people in the world, rather than the narrow vested interests of your country.

- You are more likely to recognize the influence the media has in your life.

- You are contributing to a more just world.

- You are becoming better educated, reading more widely to broaden your historical sense and your worldview.

- You understand intellectual growth as a long-term process and have designed a plan for continued development.

- You understand that your development in critical thinking will occur along a continuum, or in stages, and you chart your development accordingly.

Tips for Internalizing Each Idea

As you develop your daily or weekly plans for action, consider using one or more of the following strategies:

- Each evening, read the pages you are focused on for that day. Work the ideas into your thinking (give voice to them) so you begin to internalize them. Reread the pages until you can engage in a silent dialogue with yourself about the ideas and strategies on those pages.

- Explain the ideas you are attempting to internalize to someone else. (Ideally you would identify someone to work through these ideas with you—a significant other, perhaps.)

- Figure out the best settings for practicing the recommended strategies. Where can you best use them right away? At work? With your partner? With your children?

- Think through possible dialogues prior to actual situations. For example, if you are internalizing the idea of clarification (the idea for Day Six, "Clarify Your Thinking"), and you plan to be in a meeting on the following day, think through possible clarifying questions. For example, you might prepare to ask "Could you state that point in another way for me," "Could you give me an example of that,?" and "Would you illustrate that point for me by drawing a diagram?"

- Find ways to keep the key idea of the day in the front of your mind. You might tape a key word (such as "clarity") to the refrigerator, to your desk, or to anything else you frequently see. This will help focus your thinking on the key idea for the day.

Planning and Logging Your Progress

In the back of this section, you will find daily and weekly action plan and progress pages. Copy one set for each day or week, or write in your own notebook or journal (using the action plan and progress formats). The more time you spend giving voice to the ideas (explaining them to others, summarizing them in written form, using them explicitly in your conversations and interactions with others), the better you will internalize them, the more readily and effectively you will be able to use them, and the more spontaneous they will become.

A Caveat

As you work through this book, realize that each day's idea is a complex concept presented in simplified form. Remember our goal is to *get you started* on a path toward critical thinking. We therefore have often omitted qualifications and further commentary we would have liked to include. Furthermore, in compressing our ideas, and in seeking examples from everyday life, we may have unwittingly oversimplified some of them. What is more, you may occasionally disagree with one of our examples. If so, try not to be distracted from the larger end: your development as a thinker. Use what you can. Put aside the rest.

If one of our 30 ideas does not make sense to you, by all means pass it by and perhaps come back to it later. Give yourself time to grow, and use only those ideas you can put into action. For further explanations of the ideas, you will find recommended readings at the end of the book. We hope these ideas stimulate you to seek more and that they prompt you to make critical thinking a guiding force in your life.

Before You Begin

Before you begin to actively work through the ideas in this book, consider this idea. Then periodically revisit it:

The quality
of
your life
is
determined
by
the quality
of
your
thinking.

If humans typically form prejudices, begin with the premise that you have prejudices. If humans frequently engage in self-deception, assume you do as well. You can't make significant progress as a thinker if you maintain the myth that you are exceptional. The fact is that feeling exceptional is not at all exceptional. It is common. What *is* exceptional is the recognition that you are not exceptional—that you, like everyone else, are a self-deceived, self-centered person.

Daily Action Plan

The key idea I am focused on today is:

_____

_____

_____

_____

_____

The settings in which I can best practice using this idea are:

_____

_____

_____

_____

_____

I plan to practice using this idea in the following ways (using the following strategies):

_____

_____

_____

_____

_____

Daily Progress Notes

To be completed at the end of each day.

Today, I was successful in using the following ideas/strategies:

_____

_____

_____

The key insights that emerged for me as I attempted to take ownership of this idea were:

_____

_____

_____

One problem in my thinking I now realize I need to work on is:

_____

_____

_____

I plan to continue working on this problem in my thinking by using the following strategy:

_____

_____

_____

Some important ways in which the idea for today connects with other ideas in this book...

_____

_____

_____

Weekly Action Plan

The key idea for this week is:

_____

_____

_____

_____

_____

The settings in which I can best practice using this idea are:

_____

_____

_____

_____

_____

I plan to practice using this idea in the following ways (using these strategies):

_____

_____

_____

_____

_____

Weekly Progress Notes

To be completed at the end of each week.

This week I was successful in using the following ideas/strategies:

_____

_____

_____

The key insights that emerged for me as I attempted to take ownership of this idea were:

_____

_____

_____

One problem in my thinking I now realize I need to work on is:

_____

_____

_____

I plan to continue working on this problem in my thinking by using the following strategy:

_____

_____

_____

Some important ways in which the idea for this week connects with other ideas in this book...

_____

_____

_____

Discover Your Ignorance

Most of us assume whatever we believe to be "right." Though we were taught much of what we believe before we could critically analyze our beliefs, we nevertheless defend our beliefs as *the truth*. Good thinkers know this is absurd.

When you actively focus on uncovering your ignorance, you realize you are often wrong. You look for opportunities to test your ideas for soundness. You recognize that much of what people believe is based on prejudice, bias, half-truths, and sometimes superstition. You routinely question your beliefs. Your beliefs do not control you; you control your beliefs. You develop intellectual humility—awareness of the extent of your ignorance.

> "Willingness to be taught what we do not know is the sure pledge of growth both in knowledge and wisdom." —Blair

Intellectual humility is the disposition to distinguish, at any given moment and in any given situation, between what you know and what you don't know. People disposed toward intellectual humility recognize the natural tendency of the mind to think it knows more than it does, to see itself as right when the evidence proves otherwise. They routinely think within alternative viewpoints, making sure they are accurately representing those viewpoints. They consider other viewpoints to understand them in good faith—not to dismiss them.

Socrates, an early Greek philosopher and teacher (c. 470–399 B.C.E.), was a living model of intellectual humility. Consider:

> "Socrates philosophized by joining in a discussion with another person who thought he knew what justice, courage, or the like was. Under Socrates' questioning, it became clear that neither [of the two] knew, and they cooperated in a new effort, Socrates making interrogatory suggestions that were accepted or rejected by his friend. They failed to solve the problem, but, now conscious of their lack of knowledge, agreed to continue the search whenever possible (p. 483)."[4]

> "Profoundly sensible of the inconsistencies of his own thoughts and words and actions, and shrewdly suspecting that the like inconsistencies were to be found in other men, he was careful always to place himself upon the standpoint of ignorance and to invite others to join him there, in order that, proving all things, he and they might hold fast to that which is good (p. 332)."[5]

People with a high degree of intellectual humility (and they are rare) understand that there is far more that they will *never* know than they will *ever* know. They continually seek to learn more, to develop their intellectual abilities, and to expand their knowledge base, always with a healthy awareness of the limits of their knowledge.

Be on the lookout for...

...intellectual arrogance today, the tendency to confidently assert as true what you do not in fact know to be true. Try to discover the limitations and biases of your sources of information. Question those who speak with authority. Question the information they use in their arguments, the information they ignore, the information they distort. Question what you read and see in the media. Notice the confidence with which "the news" is asserted. Question the sources that "produce"

---

4. *Encyclopedia of Philosophy*, 1972.

5. *Encyclopedia Britannica*, Eleventh Edition, 1911, Cambridge, England: the University Press.

the news. Whenever you feel inclined to make a bold statement, stop and ask how much you really know about what you're asserting.

Strategies for developing intellectual humility:

1. When you cannot find sufficient evidence that *proves* your belief to be true, begin by saying: "I may be wrong, but what I think is…" or "Up to this point, I have believed…" or "Based on my limited knowledge in this area, I would say…".

2. Notice when you argue for beliefs without evidence to justify them. Recognize why you are doing this.

3. Actively question beliefs that seem obviously true to you, especially deeply held beliefs such as religious, cultural, or political beliefs.

4. Find alternative sources of information that represent viewpoints you have never considered.

5. Don't be afraid to "explore" new beliefs, and hence, be open to new insights.

6. Make a list of everything you absolutely know about someone you think you know well. Then make a list of things you think are true about that person, but that you cannot be absolutely sure about. Then make a list of things you do not know about that person. Then, if you can trust the person, show him or her the list to see how accurate you are. What insights emerge for you after you get feedback on such lists?

Questions you might ask to identify weaknesses in your thinking:

- What do I truly know (about myself, about this or that situation, about another person, about my nation, about what is going on in the world)?

- To what extent do my prejudices or biases influence my thinking?

- To what extent have I been indoctrinated into beliefs that might be false?
- How do the beliefs I have accepted uncritically keep me from seeing things as they are?
- Do I ever think outside the box (of my culture, nation, religion, and so on)?
- How knowledgeable am I about alternative belief systems?
- How have my beliefs been shaped by the time period in which I was born, by the place in which I was raised, by my parents' beliefs, by my spouse's beliefs, and by my religion, culture, politics, and so on?

Strive to Be a Person of Integrity: Beware of Your Own Hypocrisy

People are hypocritical in at least three ways. First, they tend to have higher standards for those with whom they disagree than they have for themselves or their friends. Second, they often fail to live in accordance with their professed beliefs. Third, they often fail to see contradictions in the behavior of people with whom they identify (such as people of high status).

Hypocrisy, then, is a state of mind unconcerned with honesty. It is often marked by unconscious contradictions and inconsistencies. Because the mind is naturally egocentric, it is naturally hypocritical. Yet at the same time, it can skillfully rationalize whatever it thinks and does. In other words, the human mind naturally wants to see itself in a positive light. The *appearance* of integrity is important to the ego-centric mind. This is why, as humans, we actively hide our hypocrisy from ourselves and from others (through self-deception and rational-ization). For example, though we are often selfish, we almost never see ourselves in this light. But we readily see selfishness in others. In other words, it is okay for me to be selfish, but not for you to be selfish. Although we expect others to adhere to much more rigid stan-dards than the standards we impose on ourselves, we see ourselves as fair. For instance, the bookkeeper who steals money from her com-pany may deceive herself into believing the company "owes" her that money, because the company has never paid her what she is worth, or, she might reason that the business is highly lucrative so should pay her more, and so on. All are rationalizations that enable her to hide from the truth. Though we profess certain beliefs, we often fail to behave in accordance with those beliefs.

Only to the extent that our beliefs and actions are consistent, only when we say what we mean and mean what we say, do we have intellectual integrity.

> "We are companions in hypocrisy."
> —William Dean Howells

When you resolve to live a life of integrity, you routinely examine your own inconsistencies and face them truthfully, without excuses. You want to know the truth about yourself. You want to know the truth in others. By facing your own hypocrisy, you begin to grow beyond it (while recognizing that you can never get full command of your hypocrisy because you can never get full command of your egocentricity). When you recognize it in others (especially those of status), they are less able to manipulate you.

See page 23 for an explanation of intellectual integrity, which is the opposite of hypocrisy.

Be on the lookout for...

...contradictions or hypocrisy in your behavior and the behavior of others today. Catch yourself using double standards. Notice when others do. Because hypocrisy is a natural human tendency, theoretically this should be easy. Look closely at what people say they believe. Compare this with what their behavior implies. Dig out inconsistencies in your thinking and behavior. Notice when you profess a belief, and then act in contradiction to that belief. Notice how you justify or rationalize inconsistencies in your behavior. Figure out the consequences of your hypocrisy. Does it enable you to get what you want without having to face the truth about yourself? Figure out the consequences of others' hypocrisies. However, if you don't see hypocrisy in yourself, look again and again and again.

Strategies for reducing hypocrisy in yourself:

- Begin to notice situations in which you expect more from others than you do from yourself. Target the areas of your greatest hypocrisy (these are usually areas in which you are emotionally involved). Do you expect more from your spouse than you do from yourself? From your coworkers? From your subordinates? From your children?

- Write a list of beliefs that seem most important to you. Then identify situations in which your behavior is inconsistent with those beliefs (where you say one thing and do another). Realize that what you believe is embedded in your actions, not your words. What does your behavior tell you about yourself? For example, you might say that you love someone while often failing to behave in accordance with his or her interests. Or, you might say your intellectual development is important to you while in fact spending little time on it.

- Think about the way you are living your life. Are you living a life of integrity where your motives are transparent? Or, are you hiding something significant? If so, what are you hiding, and more importantly, why are you doing this? How can you face your hypocrisy? What do you need to change about yourself or your situation?

Strategies for noticing hypocrisy in others:

1. Observe the people around you. Begin to analyze the extent to which they say one thing and do another. Compare their words to their deeds. For example, notice how often people claim to love someone they criticize behind the person's back. This is a common form of bad faith.

2. Think about the people you are closest to—your partner, spouse, children, or friends. To what extent can you identify hypocrisy or integrity in these relationships? To what extent do they say what they mean and mean what they say? What problems are caused by their hypocrisy?

Empathize with Others

Intellectual empathy requires us to think within the viewpoints of others, especially those we think are wrong. This is difficult until we recognize how often we have been wrong in the past and others have been right. Those who think differently from us sometimes possess truths we have not yet discovered. Practice in thinking within others' viewpoints is crucial to your development as a thinker. Good thinkers value thinking within from opposing viewpoints. They recognize that many truths can be acquired only when they "try on" other ways of thinking. They value gaining new insights and expanding their views. They appreciate new ways of seeing the world. They don't assume their perspective to be the most reasonable one. They are willing to engage in dialogue to understand other perspectives. They don't fear ideas and beliefs they don't understand or have never considered. They are ready to abandon beliefs they have passionately held when those beliefs are shown to be false or misleading.

See page 22 for a further explanation of intellectual empathy.

Be on the lookout for...

...opportunities to empathize today. Look for examples of empathetic *behavior* in others. Practice being empathetic. For example, whenever someone takes a position with which you disagree, state in your own words what you think the person is saying. Then ask the person whether you have accurately stated her or his position. Notice the extent to which others empathize with you. See whether there is a difference between what they say ("I understand") and what their behavior possibly implies (that they aren't actually listening to you). Ask someone who disagrees with you to state what he or she understands you to be saying. Notice when people distort what is being said to keep from changing their views or giving up something in their interest. Notice when you do the same. By exercising intellectual empathy, you understand others more fully, expand your knowledge of your own ignorance, and gain deeper insight into your own mind.

> "He who lives in ignorance of others lives in ignorance of himself."
> —Anonymous

Strategies for empathizing with others:

1. During a disagreement with someone, switch roles. Tell the person, "I will speak from your viewpoint for ten minutes if you will speak from mine. This will perhaps help us understand one another better." Afterward, each of you should correct the other's representation of your position: "The part of my position you don't understand is…."

2. During a discussion, summarize what another person is saying using this structure: "What I understand you to be saying is…. Is this correct?"

3. When reading, say to yourself what you think the author is saying. Explain it to someone else. Recheck the text for accuracy. This enables you to assess your understanding of an author's viewpoint. Only when you are sure you understand a viewpoint are you in a position to disagree (or agree) with it.

Deliberately Target Your Purposes

Thinking is always guided by human purposes. Everything you do is related to some purpose you have. Your purpose is whatever you try to accomplish. It is your goal or objective in any given situation or context.

Your thinking goes wrong when you aren't clear about your purpose, have unrealistic purposes, have contradictory purposes, or don't stick to your expressed purpose. Some goals are short-range and transitory; others are long-range and permanent. Some are primary. Some are secondary. Some represent your central mission in life. Others become means to other ends.

In human life, there is often a discrepancy between public (announced) goals and private (unspoken) goals. Thus, a politician's *announced* goal is usually to serve public need. The *real* goal is often to get elected, to serve ambition, and to satisfy greed.

It is important to examine the purposes that guide how you live. Which of them are you explicitly aware of? Which of them lies beneath the surface of your thinking? Which of them would you be unwilling to admit to? How many of them guide you to superficial actions? How many of them guide you to important ends? Which of them are you having difficulty accomplishing, and why?

It is also important to be able to assess others' purposes. Remembering that people's real purposes often contradict their stated purposes will enable you to see through façades and keep you from being manipulated by others.

Be on the lookout for...

...today for goals, purposes, objectives, agendas. Figure out what you are after and how you are seeking it. Determine whether your various goals are interwoven and convergent or in conflict and mutually inconsistent. Determine whether your real purposes are different from your expressed purposes. Ask yourself whether you can admit your real purposes (in this or that part of your life). Figure out what your family members, associates, and friends are after. What are their real and most basic goals? To what extent are their lives undermined by contradictory drives and aims? To what extent can they admit their real purposes? Examine personal goals, professional goals, political goals, economic goals, and social goals. Make a list of your important goals and determine whether you find inconsistencies in them.

> "There is no road to success but through a clear, strong purpose. Nothing can take its place. A purpose underlies character, culture, position, attainment of every sort."
> —T.T. Munger

Questions you can ask to target purpose:

- What exactly is my purpose in this situation?
- What am I trying to accomplish?
- Is this purpose realistic?
- Is this goal ethically justified?
- What is my most important task right now?
- What is the first thing I need to do to accomplish my purpose?
- What is the agenda of my spouse, my children, and my friends?
- How does my agenda differ from my spouse's, employees', or supervisor's?
- Does my stated agenda differ from my actual one?

- Would I be willing to admit to my true purpose in this situation? If not, why not?

Strategies for targeting purposes:

- When in a meeting, note the stated purpose and determine whether people adhere to that purpose. Notice when people wander away from the purpose and be ready with questions such as: What is our main purpose again? How is this discussion helping us achieve that purpose?

- Notice when stated purposes seem to contradict actual purposes. Intervene by saying things such as: "I believe our purpose is X. But our actions seem to imply another, contradictory purpose. How can we deal with these contradictions?"

- Think deeply about the main purposes guiding your behavior every day. Identify patterns in your behavior and then figure out the purposes (your purposes) that give rise to them in this way: "One of the main things I do is X. Therefore, my purpose, which explains X, must be Y." For instance, you might say you "want" to exercise regularly and that this is one of your goals. But then you seldom do exercise. At the same time, you rationalize your behavior—lack of exercise—by offering excuses for why you can't exercise. This implies that your real purpose is not to exercise regularly. (Your real purpose might be to convince yourself that you are doing enough to keep in shape.) Again, we should look to your behavior to determine your real purposes.

Don't Be a Conformist: Think for Yourself

Living a human life entails membership in a variety of human groups. This typically includes one's nation, culture, profession, religion, family, and peer group. We find ourselves participating in groups before we are aware of ourselves as living beings, in virtually every setting in which we function as persons. Further, every group to which we belong has a social definition of itself and unspoken "rules" that guide the behavior of all members. Each group to which we belong imposes a level of conformity on us as a condition of acceptance. This includes a set of beliefs, behaviors, requirements, and taboos.

Research shows that people, to varying degrees, accept as right and correct whatever ways of acting and believing are fostered in the social groups to which they belong. Typically, this acceptance is uncritical.

Group membership clearly offers some advantages. But those advantages can come with a price. Many people behave unethically because it is expected of them. Groups impose their rules (conventions, folkways, taboos) on individuals. (Consider the way you dress or the sexual laws in your country as obvious examples.) Group membership is, in various ways, "required" for ordinary acts of living. Suppose, for example, that you did not want to belong to any nation, that you wanted to be a citizen not of a country *but of the world*. You would not be allowed that freedom. You would find that you were allowed no place to live, nor any way to travel from place to place. Every place in the world is claimed by some a nation (as its "sovereign" possession), and every nation requires that all visitors to it come as citizens of some other country (thus, with a "passport"). In addition, everywhere a nation imposes its "sovereignty," it requires the obedience of all persons to literally thousands (if not hundreds of thousands) of laws.

For most people, blind conformity to group restrictions is automatic and unreflective. Most people effortlessly conform without recognizing their conformity. They internalize group norms and beliefs, take on the group identity, and act as they are expected to act—without the least sense that what they are doing might reasonably be questioned. Most people function in social groups as unreflective participants in a range of beliefs, attitudes, and behaviors analogous to those of urban street gangs.

Conformity is one of the evils of human society. Why? Through conformity, *arbitrary* social rules are treated as if they were *inherently* good and right. Arbitrary social rules lead to any number of unjust practices. Consider the ways in which people who do not abide by social conventions are marginalized in a culture. For example, consider the groups who tend to be marginalized in the U.S.—atheists, people who protest wars, people who speak out against unethical government practices when the mainstream is not speaking out. Furthermore, consider how arbitrary social conventions often lead to arbitrary laws, the enforcement of which often results in human suffering (for example, unjust prison sentences).

> "It is the proof of a bad cause when it is applauded by the mob."
> —Seneca

When you have developed as a skilled, independent thinker, you do not mindlessly follow the crowd. You think for yourself. You figure out for yourself what makes sense to believe and what to reject. You recognize social rules and taboos for what they often are: subjective creations of an unthinking mass.

Of course, it is often quite difficult to critically analyze the cultural conventions existing in one's own culture because these conventions are systematically indoctrinated into our thinking throughout a lifetime. As the reigning beliefs, they surround us. Overcoming indoctrination requires committed effort, insight, and courage. It implies a willingness to stand alone in your beliefs.

See page 22 for an explanation of intellectual autonomy, which is the opposite of intellectual conformity.

Be on the lookout for...

...conformity today. Assume that you are a conformist. Only when you can admit that you are a conformist can you begin to identify when and where you conform. Recognize that conformity occurs in virtually every domain of life. Look for it in the newspaper. Look for it in your relationships. Look for it in the groups to which you belong. Notice it at work. See it in others. Notice how people profess to be independent even when they are consummate conformists. Notice when you are most likely to conform (for instance, in meetings or in following the ideologies of political parties). Notice when you are least likely to conform. Figure out the consequences of your conformity. Figure out the consequences of others' conformity. Think about political conformity. Think about the consequences of nationalism (as a form of mass conformity). Figure out when it makes sense to conform (for example, not talking loudly on your cell phone while in a restaurant) and when it doesn't (for example, mindlessly supporting unethical business or governmental practices).

Strategies for becoming an independent thinker:

- Write down your answers to these questions: What are some of the taboos in my culture? What behaviors are considered *shocking* or *disgusting* (consider, for instance, sexual conventions and laws or drug laws)? What beliefs in my culture are treated as sacred? What penalties exist for people who do not abide by social rules, even though their behavior doesn't hurt anyone (and even though these rules come and go over the years)?

- Notice how taboos and rules are fostered in a culture. Note, for example, how often messages about "good" and "bad" behavior are the focus of television programs and movies. Consider, for example, the number of television programs focused on the police "catching" people in possession of illegal drugs, or the "good guys" catching the "bad guys" and locking them up. Do you find yourself cheering on the "good guys" and hoping the "bad guys get what's coming to them?" If so, why? In the real world, more harm and suffering are often caused by the official "good guys" than the official "bad guys." See if you can identify some examples.

- Examine the extent to which you uncritically accept the taboos and requirements of your culture and social groups. Monitor your conformity. Begin a list of ways in which you can begin to think independently.

- Make a list of problems that people experience as a result of mass conformity to arbitrary social rules. How do you contribute to those problems?

- Read our *Thinker's Guide to Ethical Reasoning* to get a clear understanding of the differences among ethics, social conventions, and the law. Visit www.criticalthinking.org.[6]

- Read William Graham Sumner's book *Folkways*,[7] in which he describes a broad range of societies and behaviors within varying time periods. Imagine yourself living within those various cultures. What beliefs would you hold dear? How would you behave? How would your beliefs and behaviors differ from your current beliefs and behaviors?

---

6. Paul, Richard, and Linda Elder. *The Thinker's Guide to Understanding the Foundation of Ethical Reasoning*. Dillon Beach: Foundation for Critical Thinking Press, 2006.

7. Sumner, W.G. *Folkways*. Salem, NH: Ayer Company Publishers, 1992 (originally published in 1906).

- Notice the extent to which your friends and family members conform to whatever social ideology reigns at the moment. Notice the extent to which you are stifled by the groups to which you belong (those groups you choose to belong to and those you belong to because you have no choice). Realize that independent thinkers often prefer to be alone, rather than attempt to fit into groups that irrationally and mindlessly conform to arbitrary social rules. Recognize that there is one free community you can always join—the community of independent thinkers found in the best books that have ever been written. Independent thinkers can always find a range of great thinkers waiting for them at the real or virtual library.

Clarify Your Thinking

Our own thinking usually seems clear to us, even when it is not. Vague, ambiguous, muddled, deceptive, or misleading thinking are significant problems in human

> "Muddled thinking is the key to a muddled life."
> —Anonymous

life. If you are to develop as a thinker, you must learn the art of clarifying your thinking—of pinning it down, spelling it out, and giving it a specific meaning. Here's what you can do to begin. When people explain things to you, summarize in your own words what you think they said. When you cannot do this to their satisfaction, you don't truly understand what they said. When they cannot summarize to your satisfaction what you have said, they don't truly understand what you said. Try it. See what happens.

Be on the lookout for...

...vague, fuzzy, blurred thinking—thinking that may sound good but doesn't actually say anything. Try to figure out the real meaning of what people are saying. Compare what people say with what they might really mean. Try to figure out the real meaning of important news stories. Explain your understanding of an issue to someone else to help clarify it in your own mind. Practice summarizing in your own words what others say. Then ask them if you understood them correctly. Be careful to neither agree nor disagree with what anyone says until you (clearly) understand what he or she is saying.

Strategies for clarifying your thinking:

To improve your ability to clarify your thinking (in your own mind, when speaking to others, or when writing, for example), use this basic strategy:

- State one point at a time.
- Elaborate on what you mean.
- Give examples that connect your thoughts to life experiences.
- Use analogies and metaphors to help people connect your ideas to a variety of things they already understand. (Consider this analogy: Critical thinking is like an onion. It has many layers. Just when you think you have it basically figured out, you realize there is another layer, and then another, and another, and another, and on and on.)

Here is a format you can use to make sure you are clear when speaking or writing your thoughts:

- I think (state your main point)
- In other words (elaborate on your main point)
- For example (give an example of your main point)
- To give you an analogy (give an illustration of your main point)

To clarify other people's thinking, you might ask any of the following questions:

- Can you restate your point in other words? I didn't understand you.
- Can you give an example?
- Let me tell you what I understand you to be saying. Do I understand you correctly?

As you begin to use these strategies, as basic as they seem, note how seldom others use them. Begin to notice how often people assume that others understand them when what they have said is, in fact, unintelligible, muddy, or confusing. Note how, very often, the *simple* intellectual moves are the most powerful. (For example, saying to someone: "I don't understand what you are saying. Can you say that in other words?") Focus on using these basic, foundational moves whenever it seems at all relevant to do so. As you do, you will find that your thinking becomes clearer and clearer, and you get better and better at clarifying others' thinking.

The idea of clarifying thinking is almost *so easy it is hard*. It is like watching the ball while playing tennis. It is easy to deceive ourselves into thinking we are doing it when we are not. The difference is that in tennis we get immediate feedback that tells us when we were not watching the ball (when, for instance, the ball doesn't go over the net). In thinking, we do not have this same luxury of instant feedback. So, we can remain self-deceived much of the time.

Be Relevant:
Stick to the Point

When thinking is relevant, it is focused on the main task at hand. It selects what is germane, pertinent, and related. It is on the alert for everything that connects to the issue. It sets aside what is immaterial, inappropriate, extraneous, or beside the point. That which directly bears upon (helps solve) the problem you are trying to solve is *relevant* to the problem. When thinking drifts away from what is relevant, it needs to be brought back to what truly makes a difference. Undisciplined thinking is often guided by associations ("this reminds me of that, that reminds me of this other thing") rather than what is logically connected ("if a and b are true, c must also be true"). Disciplined thinking intervenes when thoughts wander and it concentrates the mind on the things that help it figure out what it needs to figure out.

If you find your thinking digresses, try to figure out why. Is your mind simply wandering? If so, you probably need to intervene to get it back on track. Or, perhaps you realize that you need to deal with a different issue before addressing the one you were originally focused on. If so, by all means address the issue your mind has surfaced. But most importantly, *know precisely, at any given moment, the issue you are addressing,* and then stick to that issue until you have either reached resolution or made an active decision to revisit the issue later, or deal with the alternative issue that has emerged and stick to that issue. But do not allow your mind to wander aimlessly from idea to idea, issue to issue, without direction or discipline.

Be on the lookout for...

...fragmented thinking—thinking that leaps about with no logical connections. Start noticing when you or others fail to stay focused on what is relevant. Focus on finding what will help you solve a problem. When someone brings up a point that doesn't seem pertinent to the issue at hand, ask, "How is what you're saying relevant to the issue?" When working through a problem, make sure you stay focused on what sheds light on, and thus helps address, the problem. Don't allow your mind to wander to unrelated matters. Don't allow others to stray from the main issue or divert you. Frequently ask, "What is the central question? Is this or that relevant to it? How?"

> "If we are to solve a problem, we must pursue it with all our intellectual prowess, identifying exactly that which helps us solve it, and weeding out that which gets in the way." —Anonymous

Questions you can ask to make sure your thinking is focused on what is relevant:

- Am I focused on the main problem or task?
- How are these two issues connected, or are they?
- How is the problem raised intertwined with the issue at hand?
- Does the information I am considering directly relate to the problem or task?
- Where do I need to focus my attention?
- Am I being diverted to unrelated matters?
- Am I failing to consider relevant viewpoints?
- How is my point relevant to the issue I am addressing?
- What facts will actually help me answer the question? What considerations should be set aside?
- Does this truly bear on the question? How does it connect?

Be Reasonable

A hallmark of the critical thinker is the disposition to change her or his mind when given a good reason to change. Good thinkers want to change their thinking when they discover better thinking. In other words, they can and want to be *moved* by reason.

Yet, comparatively few people are reasonable in the full sense of the word. Few are willing to change their minds once set. Few are willing to suspend their beliefs to hear the views of those with whom they disagree. This is true because the human mind is not *naturally* reasonable. Reasonability, if it is to develop in the mind to any significant degree, must be actively fostered in the mind by the mind. Although we routinely make inferences or come to conclusions, we don't necessarily do so *reasonably*. Yet we typically see our conclusions as reasonable. We then want to *stick to our conclusions* without regard for their justification or plausibility. The mind typically decides whether to accept or reject a viewpoint or argument based on *whether it already believes it.*

"We think so because other people think so; or because—or because—after all, we do think so; or because we were told so, and think we must think so; or because we once thought so and think we still think so; or because, having thought so, we think we will think so." —Henry Sidgwick

To put it another way, the mind is not naturally malleable. Rather, it is, by nature, *rigid*. People often shut out good reasons readily available to them. We often refuse to hear arguments that are perfectly reasonable (when those reasons contradict what we already believe).

To become more reasonable, open your mind to the possibility, at any given moment, that you might be wrong and another person might be right. Be willing to change your mind when the situation or evidence requires it. Recognize that you don't lose anything by admitting you are wrong; rather, you gain in intellectual development.

> See page 23 to read about confidence in reason, an important intellectual trait.

Be on the lookout for...

...reasonable and unreasonable behaviors—yours and others'. Notice when you are unwilling to listen to the reasoned views of others, when you are unwilling to modify your views even when others present evidence or good reasoning that supports a better view. Carefully observe yourself. Can you be moved by reason? Are you open to the voice of reason in others? When you catch yourself being defensive, see whether you can break through your defensiveness to hear good reasons being presented. Identify times when you use language that makes you appear reasonable, even though your behavior proves otherwise. Try to figure out why you or others are being unreasonable. Do you have a selfish interest in not being open-minded? Do others have a selfish interest in not being open-minded?

Strategies for becoming more reasonable:

- Notice how seldom people admit they are wrong. Notice, instead, how often they hide their mistakes. Most people would rather lie than admit to being wrong. Decide that you do not want to be such a person.
- Say aloud, "I'm not perfect. I make mistakes. I'm often wrong." See if you have the courage to admit this during a disagreement, "Of course, I may be wrong. You may be right."

- Practice saying in your own mind, "I may be wrong. I often am. I'm willing to change my mind when given good reasons." Then look for opportunities to make changes in your thinking.

- Ask yourself, "When was the last time I changed my mind because someone gave me better reasons for his or her views than I had for mine?" To what extent are you open to new ways of looking at things? To what extent can you objectively judge information that refutes what you already think?

- Realize you are being unreasonable if:

  a. You are unwilling to listen to someone's reasons.

  b. You are irritated by reasons people give you (before thinking them through).

  c. You become defensive during a discussion.

- When you catch yourself being close-minded, analyze your thinking by completing the following statements in your journal (remember that the more details you write in your journal entries, the better able you will be to change your thinking in future similar situations):

  a. I realize I was being close-minded in this situation because…

  b. The thinking I was trying to hold onto is…

  c. Thinking that is potentially better is…

  d. This thinking is better because…

Be on the lookout for…

…opportunities to show mercy to others, to display understanding, compassion, and forgiveness. Notice the extent to which others around you favor punishment and suffering as the proper response to "deviant" behavior. Notice the extent to which you do. As you read the newspaper, notice that severe sentences often are meted out for "crimes" that injure no one except the perpetrator.

Ask yourself how often punishment is extreme (in causing human suffering). Consider "three-strikes-and-you're-out" legislation. Consider the practice of trying children as adults. Consider "adult crime, adult time" legislation (laws aimed at giving adult-length sentences to children convicted of serious crimes). Also familiarize yourself with the approach of other countries (for example, Finland) that successfully return criminals to socially meaningful lives as soon as possible, with a low rate of repeat offenders. Think of ways to deal with cultural deviance without extreme punishment and social vengeance.

Ask Deep Questions

Thinking is driven by questions. The quality of your questions determines the quality of your thinking. Superficial questions lead to superficial thinking. Deep questions lead to deep thinking. Insightful questions lead to insightful thinking. Creative questions lead to creative thinking.

Further, questions determine the intellectual tasks required of you—if you are to answer them sufficiently. For example, the question "Are there any apples in the refrigerator?" implies that, to answer the question, you need to look in the refrigerator and count the apples there. The question "What is the best way to parent in this situation?" calls on you to think about the concept of parenting, to think about the specific parenting issues you are facing at the moment, and to think about the options available to you. Thus, questions lay out different, but specific, tasks for the mind to work through.

Good thinkers routinely ask questions to understand and effectively deal with the world around them. They question the status quo. They know that things are often different from how they are presented. Their questions penetrate images, masks, fronts, and propaganda. Their questions bring clarity and precision to the problems they face. Their questions bring discipline to their thinking. Their questions show that they do not necessarily accept the world as it is presented to them. They go beyond superficial or "loaded" questions. Their questions help them solve their problems and make better decisions.

When you become a student of questions, you learn to ask powerful questions that lead to a deeper and more fulfilling life. Your questions become more basic, essential, and deep. When you understand the questions other people are asking, you can better understand their thinking and viewpoint.

Be on the lookout for...

...questions you and others ask. What types of questions do you tend to ask? When do you fail to ask important and relevant questions? Do you tend to ask deep questions or superficial ones? Listen to how others question, when they question, and when they fail to question. Examine the extent to which you are a questioner, or if you are simply one who accepts definitions of situations given by others. Focus on bringing your mind alive by improving the quality of the questions you ask. Notice the questions that guide your actions. Notice the questions that guide the actions of others.

Strategies for formulating more powerful questions:

- Whenever you don't understand something, ask a question to clarify precisely what you do not understand. Never answer a question unless you understand what it is asking.

- Whenever you are dealing with a complex problem, formulate the question you are trying to answer in several different ways (being as precise as you can) until you hit on the way that best addresses the problem at hand. Then figure out what issues, problems, or ideas you need to think through to answer the question. Figure out what information you need to consider. Do you need to look at the question from multiple viewpoints? If so, detail those viewpoints as clearly and accurately as possible before proceeding to answer the question.

> "'How do you know so much about everything?' was asked of a very wise and intelligent man; and the answer was, 'By never being afraid or ashamed to ask questions as to anything of which I was ignorant.'"
> —J. Abbott

- Whenever you plan to discuss an important issue or problem, write down in advance the most significant questions you need to address in the discussion. Be ready to change the main question if necessary. As soon as the question is clear, help those in the discussion stick to the question, making sure that the dialogue builds toward an answer that makes sense.

Questions you can ask to discipline your thinking:

- What precise question am I trying to answer?
- Is this the best question to ask in this situation?
- Is there a more important question I should be addressing?
- Does this question capture the real issue I am facing?
- Is there a question I should answer before I attempt to answer this question?
- What information do I need to gather to answer the question?
- What conclusions seem justified in light of the facts?
- What is my point of view? Do I need to consider another?
- Is there another way to look at the question?
- What are some related questions I need to consider?
- What type of question is this: an economic question, a political question, a legal question, an ethical question, or a complex question with multiple domains?

Distinguish Among Questions of Fact, Preference, and Judgment

Three Kinds of Questions

In approaching a question, it is useful to figure out what type it is. Is it a question with one definitive answer? Is it a question that calls for a subjective choice? Or does the, question require us to consider competing answers?

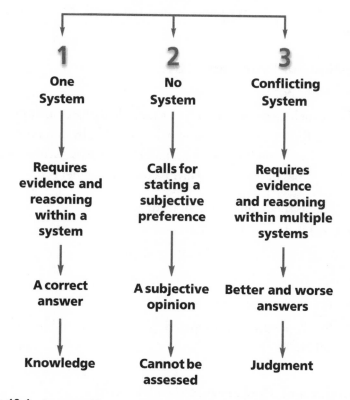

Figure 10.1   In approaching a question, it is useful to figure out what type it is. Is it a question with one definitive answer? Is it a question that calls for subjective choice? Or, does the question require us to consider competing answers?

One way to analyze questions is to focus on the type of reasoning required by the question. With one-system questions, there is an established procedure or method for finding the answer. With no-system questions, the question is properly answered in accordance with one's subjective preference; there is no "correct" answer. With conflicting-system questions, there are multiple competing viewpoints from which and within which one might reasonably pursue an answer

> "To every complex question there is a simple answer and it is wrong...."
> —H.L. Mencken

to the question. There are better and worse answers, but no verifiable "correct" ones, because even experts often disagree on how to approach them or answer them (hence, the "conflict" from system to system).

Questions of Procedure (Established or One-System)

These include questions with an established procedure or method for finding the answer. They are settled by facts, by definition, or by both. They are prominent in math and the sciences. Everyone deals with these types of questions daily. Examples include:

- What is the boiling point of lead?
- What is the size of this room?
- What is the differential of this equation?
- How does the hard drive on a computer operate?
- What is the sum of 659 and 979?
- How is potato soup prepared, according to established Polish tradition?

Questions of Preference (No System)

These are questions with as many answers as there are different human preferences (a category in which subjective taste rules). Answers to these questions can be, if you will, anything you like, as long as they are relevant to the question. Consequently, it wouldn't make sense to judge people for their preferences. Examples include:

- Which would you prefer, a vacation in the mountains or one at the seashore?
- How do you like to wear your hair?
- Do you like to go to the opera? Which is your favorite?
- What color scheme do you prefer in your house?
- What is your favorite restaurant?

Questions of Judgment (Conflicting Systems)

These are questions requiring reasoning, but with more than one arguable answer. These are questions that make sense to debate, questions with better-or-worse answers (well-supported and reasoned or poorly-supported and/or poorly-reasoned). For these questions, we seek the best answers within a range of possibilities.

Answers to these questions should be evaluated using universal intellectual standards such as clarity, accuracy, and relevance. These questions are predominant in the human disciplines (history, philosophy, economics, sociology, art, and so on). Many everyday questions related to parenting, intimate relationships, economics, and politics are questions of judgment. Examples include:

- How can we best address the most basic and significant economic problems of the nation today?
- What can be done to significantly reduce the number of people who become addicted to harmful drugs?
- How can we balance business interests and environmental preservation?
- How progressive should the tax system be?
- Should capital punishment be abolished?
- What is the best economic system?

- What is the best way to approach this client, given the complexities in the issues?

People tend to be better at figuring out answers to questions of fact or procedure than questions of judgment. People often want to simplify the thought process by looking for the "right" answer. But many of the important questions in life cannot be answered so easily. How does it make sense to parent this particular child? What is the best way to work with this difficult employee? What do I want in a marriage? How do we significantly reduce the amount of destruction to the planet caused by humans? What health care system should I support? How do we bring about peace in the Middle East? All these are questions of judgment and, as such, require us to reason within multiple, conflicting viewpoints.

Be on the lookout for...

...confusion between these three types of questions in the thinking of others. Look for the same confusion in your thinking. As you go through the day, practice identifying these different types of questions. Identify them in your own thinking as well as in the thinking of others. Notice when you (erroneously) assert a factual answer to a question that is not a question of fact, but one requiring reasoned judgment. Notice the same tendency in others. When thinking through a question of judgment, identify all the important and relevant viewpoints and articulate those viewpoints as accurately as possible, especially those with whom you disagree.

Strategies for internalizing and using the three types of questions:

- Just by understanding these three distinct types of questions, you can immediately apply your understanding of them in your everyday life. When in a meeting, notice the main types of questions people discuss. Are these questions focused on complex questions of judgment? Are the questions mainly factual? Are people talking about their preferences?

- Begin to notice when people treat questions of judgment as questions of fact or procedure. For instance, notice when people dogmatically assert their views as "facts" rather than as one possible way to reason through a complex question of judgment. Notice whether (and to what extent) people seem able to enter, in good faith, multiple viewpoints relevant to questions of judgment.

- At the end of the day, make a list of the important questions you reasoned through that day. Then categorize them. Were they mainly questions of fact or procedure? Were they mainly questions of preference? Of judgment? Then, how did you address each one? Did you look for a simple answer to a question of judgment? Did you ask someone to give his or her reasoning in answer to a question of preference (when you shouldn't have)?

Think Through Implications

All thinking has an internal dynamic. It leads somewhere and, when acted upon, has consequences. You can't be a critical thinker if you are insensitive to the many implications inherent in your thinking. Likewise, you can't be a critical thinker if you ignore the

> "Fools measure actions after they are done, by the event; wise men beforehand, by the rules of reason."
> —Richard Hill

consequences in your life that follow from the thinking that is driving your thinking. Focus on where your thinking is leading you.

What are some important consequences of…

- …the food you eat (and the food you don't eat)?
- …the amount of exercise you do?
- …how you spend your time?
- …the emotions you feed and those you ignore?
- …fear, anger, envy, and jealousy in your life?

When you consider the implications of what you might do before you do it, you explicitly choose (insofar as you can) the consequences that happen when you act. Some people simply don't imagine what will or might follow when they act on a decision they have made. They smoke cigarettes but are unprepared for lung problems. They don't exercise but are unprepared for muscle deterioration. They don't actively develop their minds but are unprepared for the increasing inflexibility and close-mindedness that come with aging when one fails to do this. They don't realize that everything they do has implications. They don't realize that it is possible to make a habit of thinking through the implications of decisions *before* acting, and thus learn to act more wisely, to live more rationally. Critical, reflective thinkers actively consider the implications of their actions before acting and modify their behavior accordingly (before they experience negative consequences).

Not only are there implications for your decisions, but implications are embedded in what you say, in the words you decide to use. That is, the way you use language implies specific things. For example, if you say to your wife, in a loud and angry tone, "Why the hell didn't you do the dishes?," you imply, at a minimum:

- She should have done the dishes.
- She knows that she should have done the dishes.
- She knew you would be upset if she didn't do the dishes.
- In the future, under similar circumstances, she better do the dishes unless she wants you to get angry and shout at her.

Because implications are connected with or follow from everything you say, choose your words carefully. Before you say anything, be sure you have thought through the implications of your words. Resolve to use language with care and precision.

Be on the lookout for...

... implications of decisions or potential decisions—your decisions and those of others. Look on the surface for obvious implications. Look beneath the surface for less-obvious implications. Notice the implications of what you say. Look closely at the consequences of your actions. Make a list of all the significant implications of a potential decision before acting. Notice when others fail to think through implications. Look for examples in the newspaper. Notice that some decisions have insignificant results, whereas others (such as a decision to go to war) lead to deadly results and damaged lives. Look for opportunities to help others think through implications (your children or your significant other, for example, or your colleagues or employees).

Strategies for thinking through implications:

- Look at your life as a set of moment-to-moment options. At any moment, you can do X, Y, or Z. Every act, and every pattern of actions, has outcomes. What outcomes do you want? What must you do to anticipate likely outcomes? The answer is to become a student of your own behavior, reflect on the likely outcomes of possible decisions, and make your decisions more mindfully.

- When faced with a difficult problem, make a list of the likely implications of dealing with the problem in various ways. Then act in the way that is likely to lead to the best outcome in the circumstances.

- Think about the implications (for future health and happiness) of the way you are now living your life. Make a list of the implications you probably will face if you continue to to live as you are. Will you be satisfied with those implications? Concentrate on the likely negative implications of your habits.

- Carefully observe the language you use when framing your thoughts. Note what is implied by what you say. Note also what is implied by what others say. How do others react to what you say to them? Make a commitment to carefully choose your words before speaking to others—be aware of what you might imply.

Questions you should ask to target implications:

- If I decide to do X, what is likely to happen?
- If I decide *not* to do X, what is likely to happen?
- If we make this decision in this relationship, what are the likely implications? What were the consequences when we made similar decisions before?
- What are the implications of ignoring a specific problem (for example, in an intimate relationship or in parenting)?
- If I keep living in the present as I have in the past, what consequences will I likely face?

Distinguish Inferences from Assumptions

People often confuse inferences with assumptions. But it is
important to clearly distinguish
between these two elements or
parts of reasoning. An inference
is a step of the mind, in which the

"A wise man proportions
his belief to the
evidence."
—David Hume

mind says, "This is true; therefore, that is true." The conclusion, or
inference, that something is true is based on something else being
true, or appearing true. People routinely make inferences throughout
the day. And these inferences can be justified or unjustified. All inferences are based on assumptions—that is, beliefs we take for granted.
Justifiable assumptions lead to reasonable inferences. Assumptions
usually operate at the unconscious level. When we uncover our
assumptions, we often find the roots of prejudice, stereotyping, bias,
and other forms of irrational thinking.

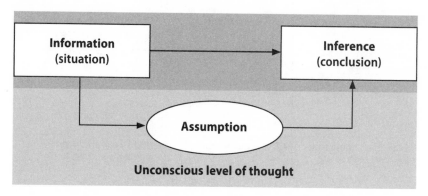

Consider these examples focused on distinguishing inferences from assumptions:

Example 1:

Situation: My nation is in a conflict with another nation.

Inference: My nation is justified in this conflict.

Assumption: My nation is always justified in its conflicts with other nations.

Example 2:

Situation: My spouse spends considerable time with her male supervisor outside of work.

Inference: She is having an affair with her supervisor.

Assumption: Whenever a woman spends considerable time with her male supervisor outside of work, she is having an affair with him.

The following method (outlined in Table 12.1) identifies inferences and assumptions in your thinking. First determine what you might infer (either rationally or irrationally) in a situation. Then determine the specific generalization, or belief, that leads to the inference. This is the assumption.

Information (Situation)	Possible <u>Inference</u> One Might Make	<u>Assumption</u> Leading to the Inference
1. You see a person throwing trash out of the window of a moving car.	1. That person is ignorant as to the implications of littering.	1. Whenever a person throws trash out of the window of a moving car, he or she is ignorant as to the implications of littering.
2. You see a person with a black eye.	2. That person has been hit by someone.	2. Whenever a person has a black eye, he or she has been hit by someone.
3. You see a child crying next to her mother in the grocery store.	3. The mother has refused to get the child something she wants.	3. Whenever a child is crying next to her mother in the grocery store, the mother has refused to give the child something she wants.
4. You see a man sitting on a curb with a paper bag in his hand.	4. The man must be a bum.	4. All men sitting on curbs with paper bags in their hands are bums.

When you explicitly identify inferences, and then figure out the assumptions leading to those these inferences, you gain more control over your thinking and therefore your life. You begin to uncover the assumptions, the beliefs you take for granted, that are guiding your actions. If, for instance, you assume that all supervisors are arbitrary, controlling people, this is what you will see in every supervisor you have. If you take for granted that the industrial pollution caused by your company doesn't cause health problems, you won't be motivated to check this assumption to see if it is justified, given the evidence. If you assume your spouse will always be there for you no matter how badly you treat him or her, you might be in for a surprise later on.

People often say, "I assume X is true, or I assume X," when what they actually mean is "I infer X is true," or "I infer X." If they assumed it, they probably wouldn't state it; they would take it for granted and therefore wouldn't think it needs to be stated. They would likely think that others shared their view as well (and therefore, would not check their assumptions with those other people). Remember that assumptions usually lie at the unconscious level of thought and are therefore not always easily accessible.

Be on the lookout for...

...people confusing inferences with assumptions. Also notice how often people seem unaware of their inferences and assumptions. Notice when you use the word "assumptions" or "assume." Notice when others use these words. Notice when you use the term "inferences" or "infer." Figure out whether you, or others, are using these terms correctly.[8] Work on ferreting out your assumptions by first noticing your inferences.

---

8. See *inference* and *assumption* in the glossary of terms.

Strategies for taking command of your inferences and assumptions:

- To practice distinguishing inferences from assumptions, create your own situations. Then, formulate an inference someone might make, either justifiably or not, in that situation (X is true; therefore, Y is true). Finally, determine the precise assumption that leads to the inference.

Situation	Possible Inference One Might Make	Assumption Leading to the Inference
1.		
2.		
3.		
4.		

- Practice distinguishing inferences from assumptions throughout the day, just to get the basic strategy down. Use a strategy like the one above. Begin to notice, first your inferences, and second your assumptions, in this way: "Right now, in this situation, I am inferring X; I am pretty sure this inference comes from this assumption…" Don't be concerned with how profound or superficial your inferences and assumptions seem. Just work toward understanding this process as it is occurring in your mind: situation, then inference, and then assumption.

(situation → inference → assumption)

Note that though the assumption leads to the inference, to identify it, we approach it backwards. We look for the inference first because it lies more readily at the conscious level of thought. Hence, it is easier to identify it.

• When you have mastered this basic strategy, target the important inferences you make. What important inferences are you making about your career, your marriage, a big issue at work, your parenting, other sentient creatures, the prison system, capitalism, and so on.

Don't Be Fooled by the Words People Use: Look Underneath Words to Unspoken Realities

We tend to have very little understanding of the role words play in how we experience reality. From the beginning of life, we are immersed in words, language, and ideas. For example, parents point to an object or person and say the associated word to the child—this is a *chair*. This is a *spoon*. This is *Mommy, Daddy, baby, bad, good, nice, mean, ugly, pretty*. With these, and many other, words we form beliefs. ("I am *good*." "I have the *best Mommy and Daddy*." "Some people are *bad*." "These kinds of things are *ugly* or *disgusting*.") Because of our native sociocentricity, we often form our beliefs in accordance with approval or disapproval. We tend to uncritically assume the approved views of society.

> "A picture held us captive. And we could not get outside it, for it lay in our language and language seemed to repeat it to us inexorably."
>
> —Ludwig Wittgenstein

As we grow and age, we form ideologies, perspectives, and world-views, based on the words and meanings we put together in our minds in their various configurations. These beliefs, based in words, form the fabric of our minds; they determine how we see the world, the assumptions we formulate, and the theories we use to figure things out.

We often choose words to serve our selfish interests or maintain our sociocentric viewpoint. The concept of *doublespeak*, which refers to the use of language to deliberately disguise or distort the root meaning of words, colorfully illustrates this point. Consider the following examples:[9]

- The term *collateral damage* covers up the reality of *innocent people being killed* during war.
- Children in our country are taught to *understand the world as it is,* whereas Cuban (or Russian, or Iranian, or Libyan) children are *brainwashed* (into cultural ideologies).
- Politicians aren't *spending* taxpayer money; they are *investing* it for the future.
- We are *freedom fighters*; they are *terrorists*—though we both engage in similar unethical behavior.
- We stand for *justice*; they are for *oppression*.
- We are *self-confident,* whereas they (whoever opposes us) are *arrogant*.
- When our allies suffer loss of life at an enemy's hands, we call it an *attack* in cold blood; when our enemies suffer loss of life at our hands, we call it *retaliation*.
- The U.S. Government uses the term *rendition* to refer to people it illegally kidnaps and imprisons in foreign countries, beyond the reach of the law, in order to torture them if our government deem it *necessary* (because U.S. laws forbid such torture on U.S. ground).
- We call farm animals *livestock* rather than, for instance, *animals we kill to eat.* We use the terms *meat* and *steak* and *poultry* rather than *dead animal flesh.* (Imagine ordering dead animal flesh at a restaurant.)

---

9. Some of these examples were taken from www.newspeakdictionary.com, June 11, 2012.

Consider, as well, the following verbal disguises:

- We sometimes say, "I love you," when our behavior implies "you'll do until someone better comes along."

- We sometimes say, "I need my freedom," when our behavior implies "I don't want to accept responsibility for my own children."

- We sometimes say, "No one is perfect," when our behavior implies "I am obscuring much more than occasional peccadillos."

- We sometimes say, "I need more love," when our behavior implies "I need more sex."

- We sometimes say, "She is a loose woman," when her behavior simply implies "she is exploring her sexuality in nonconventional ways."

- We sometimes say, "I just like foods that taste good" when our behavior implies "I am addicted to unhealthy foods."

- We sometimes say, "I'm trying to save money," when our behavior implies "I am addicted to shopping."

The words we choose determine how we think of "reality." If you don't go along with the unreasonable thinking of your colleagues, for instance, you might be considered "uncooperative." To "cooperate," according to this logic, means accepting the thinking of the group, however irrational.

Consider the use of "waterboarding," which has been used by the U.S. government to torture people considered "enemies." Waterboarding, which sounds like something fun you might do with a surfboard in the ocean, is actually a label for the act of pouring water into a person's face while he is lying on his back, to take him to the brink of drowning, and doing this repeatedly. By using a term like "waterboarding," we can obscure the fact that we are torturing people. The torture is camouflaged and minimized. We can foster a positive image of ourselves and hide the gruesome reality.

In brief, your behavior comes predominantly from your conceptualizations of reality and how you see yourself relating to those realities (through your conceptualizations).[10] These conceptualizations are deeply connected to the words you choose.

Critical thinkers are meticulous in their word choice. If they say, "I *love* you," you can readily see love implicit in their actions toward you. If they say, "I am trying to *live the examined life*," you can see them living more and more rationally over time. Critical thinkers try to mirror, or conceptualize, in their minds what is truly happening. They try to use the words that capture what is truly happening. They command their behavior through the words they choose. For example, "I am in charge of my life." "I make the decisions that determine my future." "I am the captain of my ship." They recognize that self-deception often causes them to conceptualize things in ways that serve their interests rather than the truth.

Be on the lookout for...

...the misuse of words. Notice when others use words to favor their interests or advantage. Notice when people use words in ways that don't fit what is truly happening. Look for explanations that don't seem accurate or logical. Examine the words you choose. Do you choose words to situate things so you can (selfishly) get more for you? To better understand situations and people, mentally strip the words off the things and try to see what is truly there. General semanticists tell us: *The word is not the thing.* When we internalize this insight, we have a powerful tool for gaining command of our definitions and, consequently, our lives.

---

10. It might be helpful here to recognize that *the concept of a concept is a difficult concept to teach.* We must use ideas to explain ideas. We rely on concepts to understand other concepts: hence the difficult nature of the material for today (or this week). Refer to the glossary term for *concept* at the back of the book as a starting place. Also see the recommended readings in the back of the book. Further, see John Wilson's book, *Thinking with Concepts* (1970).

Strategies for choosing words more carefully:

- When in a disagreement with someone, state as accurately as possible (in good faith) that person's viewpoint. Notice the words you use to describe his or her viewpoint. Identify different words that might better capture the viewpoint. Present your articulation to the person you are in disagreement with, if you can. Ask whether your words adequately capture this person's viewpoint. If not, rearticulate the viewpoint until the other person is satisfied.

- Notice yourself using words in ways that are irrational or that hide what is actually happening in your thinking. What are you hiding from? What are you trying not to see in your thinking? What are you trying not to face about something in your life? For instance, people who feel trapped in their work situation often use language that in essence keeps them trapped. Instead of using words that trap you, use words that free you. Instead of saying, "There is nothing I can do to change my situation," say rather, "There is something I can do to change my situation. I just need to figure out what that is and start moving in that direction." The first way of talking traps you; the second sets you free.

- Notice the way others use words. Notice when they use words in ways not reasonably justifiable in context.

- Notice when people use words in ways that get them more of what they want without having to consider the rights of others. (An example is when people say they "need" things when they actually just "want" them. This is a common phenomenon in capitalistic countries that leads to overproduction of certain products and the waste of Earth's resources.)

- Notice when people use words in demeaning ways. For instance, for more than 100 years, homophobic people have used derogatory words and expressions in referring to homosexuals—such as *queer, homo, that way, a bit funny, a friend of Dorothy,* and so on. These words then hold them hostage, defining their perspectives on homosexuality and sometimes leading to "hate crimes" or other unethical behavior.

• When in a disagreement with someone, instead of giving your interpretation (conceptualization) of the situation, just state the facts. Instead of saying, "You always do X and you never do Y," say, "This is what I see happening in this situation. Here are the facts. Do you agree with the facts as I have stated them? What is the most reasonable way to interpret these facts?" Be open to the possibility that you are misrepresenting the facts as you go through this exercise, especially if your ego is involved.

• Try to become keenly aware of your word choice. Make every word you say represent the truth or the situation as well as possible. Notice how few people have this level of command of their words, and therefore, their thoughts and the quality of their life.

When You Think You Have Arrived as a Critical Thinker, Think Again

One of the great barriers to the creation of fairminded critical societies is that all of us see ourselves as fairminded critical thinkers. We all see ourselves, when it comes right down to it, as the source of ultimate truth. In other words, to get to the truth, just ask me. We assume our way of thinking to be best, our values the highest, our perspective the most well-rounded. Republicans and Democrats alike see themselves as critical thinkers. Atheists and Christians, teachers and administrators, employers and the employed, husband and wife, parent and (at least grown) child—all see themselves as critical thinkers.

> "What we hope ever to do with ease, we must learn first to do with diligence."
> —Samuel Johnson

The tendency to lack insight into our ignorance, as we have already pointed out, is part and parcel of the human mind. Everyone has this tendency, whatever his or her level of intellectual skill or ability. The phenomenon is similar in us all, from highly trained medical doctors and scientists, to factory workers and farmhands.

Though the development of critical thinking requires diligent practice and deep commitment, as does the development of any complex skill set, people tend to think their thinking is good enough without practice. Most people readily admit, if asked, that they know little or nothing about what it takes to play the violin, because they have never studied it. But they do not take the same approach to thinking. They would not say that they know little or nothing about thinking because they haven't studied it. Instead, they would uncritically defend their thinking.

The problem is that thinking, the cultivation of fairminded critical thinking, is not studied seriously enough in human societies. Critical thinking is rarely discussed as such. The term "critical thinking" is bandied about but seldom authentically explored. If you ask most people to define critical thinking, they would draw more or less a blank. They might give a partial or vague answer. They might see critical thinking as something like a formulaic approach to problem solving.

Consider critical thinking to be something you can only imperfectly understand, because there is always another layer. In other words, critical thinking should be understood as something we aspire to, but can never fully achieve. Because we are largely egocentric and sociocentric thinkers, we can never be master or ideal critical thinkers.

Be on the lookout for...

...the use of the term "critical thinking." Notice how people often use it in connection with what they already believe, even though their beliefs are not sound. Notice how rarely people explain their conception of critical thinking. Notice how people tend to assume their thinking to be reasonable, however illogical. Notice how people in the professions often automatically assume that those in their profession, or their division or department, think critically.

Strategies for continuing to develop as a critical thinker:

- Make a list of all the areas of your life in which you would say you are a critical thinker. For each of these, identify weaknesses in your thinking. If you don't find any, dig further.
- Make a list of the areas in your life in which you would definitely say you are not a critical thinker or not as good at critical

thinking as in other areas of your life. Identify precisely what is wrong with your thinking. Remember that the more details you include, the more likely you will be to identify and address the problems.

- Notice when others use the term "critical thinking." Ask them for their definition of critical thinking to see whether it seems substantive.

- Reconcile yourself to being an imperfect thinker at best, but commit to gradual improvement over the long run.

- Write a journal entry, a letter to yourself, in which the most reasonable side of you is given voice: "Theoretically, I want to be a critical thinker. I want to take command of my thoughts, feelings, and desires. But I still find myself doing... I still engage in the following irrational behaviors... I continue to... Nevertheless, I am beginning to notice..."

Be Fair, Not Selfish

Human thinking is naturally self-serving or selfish. Selfishness is a *native*, not learned, human tendency (though it can be encouraged or discouraged by one's culture and the groups to which one belongs). Humans naturally tend to look out for "number one." Unfortunately, that often means we are unfair to persons "two" and "three."

> "Selfishness is that detestable vice which no one will forgive in others, and no one is without in himself."
> —H.W. Beecher

You don't have to be selfish. It is possible to develop as a fair person and thinker. You can learn to give significant attention to the desires, needs, and rights of others. You do not need to "cheat yourself" to be fair.

When you think fairmindedly, you consider the rights and needs of others as equivalent to your own. You forego the pursuit of your desires when fair play requires it. You learn how to overcome your selfishness. You learn how to step outside your point of view and into others' points of view. You value fairmindedness as a personal characteristic worth pursuing.

See page 23 for an explanation of fairmindedness.

Be on the lookout for...

...selfishness today—in yourself and others. Notice how often people justify their selfishness. Notice how often they object to the selfishness of others. Look closely at the role of selfishness in your life. Note how hard it is to be fair to those you have been taught to consider "evil." Note how difficult it is to identify your own unfair behavior (because the mind naturally hides what it doesn't want to face).

Strategies for developing as a fairminded thinker:

- Recognize anew, every day, that you, like every other human, are *naturally* self-centered—that you, like every other human, are primarily interested in how the world and everything in it can serve you. Only by bringing this idea to the forefront of your thinking can you begin to get command of your selfishness and self-centered tendencies.

- Be on the alert to catch yourself in the mental act of self-deception—for example, ignoring others' viewpoints. Remember that all humans engage in some self-deception. Exceptional persons recognize this tendency in themselves and consistently work to take command of it.

- Log each time you do something selfish. Reward yourself for noticing your selfishness and not letting yourself off the hook. Target the excuses you use to rationalize self-serving behavior. Write down in detail how and when you are selfish. Then write down the point of view of those who are affected by your selfishness. Consider how you can avoid such behavior in future similar situations. You might use the following format to log your selfish episodes:
  - Today I was selfish in the following way...
  - My selfish (but unspoken) thinking was as follows... Be as honest as possible. Do not allow your mind to get away with self-deception as you detail your thinking.
  - My selfishness affected the following person or people in the following way(s)...
  - In the future, I can avoid being selfish or self-centered in a similar situation by thinking and behaving in the following rational ways...

- Take every opportunity you can to think broadly about issues that involve multiple viewpoints. Assume that your mind will tend to favor whatever perspective you hold in any given situation. Force your mind, if necessary, to consider other relevant ways of looking at the issue or situation (and to represent those viewpoints accurately, rather than in a distorted way).

Questions you can ask to foster fairness in your thinking:

- Am I being fair to… right now?

- Am I putting my *desires* ahead of the *rights* and *needs* of others? If so, what precisely am I after and whose rights or needs am I ignoring or violating?

- When I think about the way I live, how often do I put myself in others' shoes?

- Do I have a selfish interest in not seeing the truth in this situation? If I face the truth, will I have to change my behavior?

- Do I think broadly enough to be fair? How many alternative perspectives have I explored? What national, religious, political, ideological, and social points of view have I considered?

- In what types of situations do I tend to be selfish? With my spouse? My children? My friends? My coworkers?

Get Control of Your Emotions

People are often confused about the role emotions play in life. For example, in our culture, they frequently place people in one of two categories: thinkers or feelers. Consequently, they might make the following kind of state-

> "Emotion turning back on itself, and not leading on to thought or action, is an element of madness..."—J. Sterling

ment: "The problem in our relationship is that you are a thinker and I feel things. I am an emotional person. You aren't." But differentiating between thinkers and feelers is a conceptual mistake. As humans, all of us think, and all of us experience emotions throughout the day, every day.

At this very moment, you are thinking something, feeling something, and wanting something. You are thinking about what you are reading. You feel some emotion, which comes from your interpretation of the ideas you are reading. And you are motivated to read on, or not, given how you think and what you feel. This occurs time and time again throughout the day.

Cognition (thinking) and affect (feelings and desires) are two sides of the same coin. If you think, for example, that someone has been unjust to you, you will feel some negative emotion (such as anger or resentment) toward that person. The feeling happens in the mind as a result of how you think in the situation. Moreover, feelings can usefully influence and drive thought. For example, if you are angry about something you think is unjust, your anger can drive you to think about what you can do to eliminate the injustice.

Feelings and emotions, then, are an essential part of your make-up. They can be positive or negative. They signal whether you perceive ideas in a positive or negative light. They can be justified or unjustified. How you relate to your emotions can make a big difference in the quality of your life. You can feed or starve a given emotion. You can use your emotions to drive you toward good or ill. As you examine your emotions more closely, investigate the thinking that accounts for them. You can attack thinking that leads to self-inflicted unproductive emotional pain. You can take command of your emotions by taking command of the thinking that causes those emotions.

See pages 24-27 for useful diagrams on this idea.

Be on the lookout for...

...feelings and emotions—your emotions and the emotions of others. Look on the surface, at the emotions you can easily see. Look beneath the surface, for the emotions you would deny you feel. Notice how people often justify their own negative emotions. Notice how they often object to the negative emotions of others. Notice how we tend to invalidate the emotions of those we consider beneath us or those whose views we don't share. Look closely at the role of emotions in your life. Realize that even negative emotions can serve a useful role in your development. If you are doing things to hurt others, you should feel bad about what you are doing. Do not confuse the feelings of a healthy conscience with the emotions of egocentricity. Every time you feel a negative emotion, stop and ask yourself: "Why? What thoughts or behavior are leading to this feeling?" Resolve to attack unproductive thinking with productive thinking—which should lead to productive feelings.

Strategies for taking command of your emotional life:

- Begin to notice the emotions you regularly experience. Every time you experience a negative emotion, ask yourself: "What

thinking is leading to this emotion?" See whether you can identify some irrational thinking underlying the emotion. If so,
attack that thinking with better, more sensible thinking. Once
you act on the new thinking, your emotion should begin to shift
accordingly.

- If you experience negative emotions frequently in your life,
  look closely at what is causing these emotions. Is it you? Is your
  irrational thinking leading to unproductive behavior? Are you
  in a dysfunctional relationship that you need to get out of? Is it
  your job? Until you directly face the problems in your life that
  are causing negative emotions, and until you do something to
  change the situation, the negative emotions will keep coming
  back. Get to the root of the emotions. Don't ignore the issues
  until you have fully dealt with the problems. Attack your mind
  with thinking that leads to productive behavior and positive
  emotions.

- To focus more concretely on your emotions, write about them.
  Target the negative emotions in your journal. Use the following
  format:
  - One negative emotion I feel is...
  - The reason I feel this negative emotion is...
  - The thinking (or situation) I need to change in order not
    to feel this negative emotion is...
  - A more productive way to think is to ask yourself, "If I
    change the way I think, my feelings should change in the
    following ways..."

This strategy is focused on negative emotions. By analyzing what
is giving rise to negative emotions, you can often identify problems
in your thinking and behavior. If you don't experience many negative emotions, there can be a number of reasons why. For example,
it might be that you are living a predominantly rational life, and therefore you experience the positive emotions that come with reasonable,
unselfish living. Or it might be that you are satisfied and happy with
your life because you are good at manipulating others (that is, at

getting what you want without having to change). For example, the successful dominator primarily feels positive emotions (see Day Seventeen, "Take Control of Your Desires"). It is up to you to determine the truth about your emotional life.

Take Control of Your Desires

If you want to be in command of your life, you have to get command of the desires that direct your behavior. Otherwise, it is all too easy to pursue irrational

"No man is free who cannot control himself."—Pythagoras

desires—desires that are self-destructive or harmful to others, such as the desire to dominate. When you don't actively assess and critique what you want, you often end up pursuing senseless desires without knowing why.

When you develop as a self-reflective thinker, you can differentiate between desires that make sense and those that don't, between those that can be justified and those that can't. You work to reject desires that lead to suffering. You break down habits that feed self-destructive desires. You establish habits conducive to a fulfilling life. Recognizing that much suffering results from the unbridled pursuits of greed, power, or approval, you carefully monitor these natural, but harmful, human desires in yourself. You simplify your life. Realizing that most irrational desires function at the unconscious level of thought, you work to bring your them out into the open to examine them. You explicitly formulate your purposes, goals, and motives so you can more easily assess them.

It is important to realize that desires function in relation to thoughts and feelings. Wherever you have desires, your thinking leads to those desires. You experience feelings when you act on those desires. For example, if you desire, or *want*, to move to a different job, you *think* that the job will be better than your current job in one or more ways. When you begin working at the new job, you then *feel* some emotions as a result (for example, satisfaction, dissatisfaction, fulfillment, or frustration). If you *feel* dissatisfied, you might be *driven* to *rethink* your decision. You might try to go back to your old job. And so it goes.

Thus, each of the mind's three functions—thoughts, feelings, and emotions—continually interact and influence one another. Critical thinkers understand the relationship among thoughts, feelings, and desires. They routinely assess the desires guiding their behavior. They analyze the thinking that gives rise to those desires.

See pages 24-27 for useful diagrams.

Be on the lookout for...

...desires today—your desires and the desires of others. Notice how often people pursue irrational desires. Identify which of your desires you can admit and which you try to hide. Notice how often people try to justify self-serving desires. Notice how they object to the self-serving desires of others. Look closely at the implications of desires in your life. Every pursuit has its price. Notice how the pursuit of wealth, power, status, and celebrity impacts the quality of life—for you and others. Much suffering and injustice result from them. You can never be a reasonable or just person if you are subservient to selfish or irrational desires.

Strategies for controlling your desires:

- Recognize that every action you take is driven by your purpose or desire. Make a list of every behavior you engage in that leads to humiliation, pain, or suffering, or that is dysfunctional in some other way (to yourself or others). For every behavior on your list, write a detailed explanation of why you engage in this behavior. Question each explanation: What motivates you? You might have to do some digging here, because your egocentric mind tries to convince you that you have no irrational desires.

- Think through the implications of each behavior you just listed. Detail in writing what happens, or might happen, as a result of each behavior. Be as specific as possible. Again, don't hide from the truth.

- List some things you can do immediately to alter your dysfunctional behavior (remember that your behavior comes from your desires). Your behavior is probably influenced by your situation. Reflect on the questions: Do you need to change some things in your situation? Do you need to move? Do you need to get out of a bad relationship? Do you need to learn better coping strategies? Do you need to read the ideas in this section once a week to be reminded of useful strategies for targeting unreasonable desires?

- Write a detailed plan for changing your dysfunctional behavior. The more details you include, the more useful your plan will be.

Don't Dominate Others: Don't Be a Top Dog

Dominating behavior entails controlling or using power over others to serve your interest, without regard to the rights and needs of others. We might also call this "top dog" behavior. Many problems in human life stem from the human tendency to dominate others. It is obvious in those who bully. Domination is often indirect and therefore difficult to detect. Human domination through manipulation plays a central role in modern society. It almost always harms, at some level, those being controlled. Tremendous suffering results from this tendency.

> "Hateful is the power, and pitiable is the life, of those who wish to be feared rather than to be loved."
> —Cornelius Nepos

Unfortunately, people who are successful at dominating others, people who can get others to do what they want through direct control, power, or manipulation, might be among those least likely to change. This is true because "successful" dominators tend to experience positive emotions. They usually see things as going well for them. They like their life and tend to think that their relationships are generally good (even when others in those relationships are unhappy). If you are such a person, you will have to work harder to change (than someone who experiences the negative consequences of his or her controlling behavior). You will have to change, not because you experience emotional pain or obvious problems in relationship to others, but because you recognize the unethical nature of dominating behavior.

Rational persons do not want to dominate others, even when they can get away with it, and even when they personally benefit from their controlling behavior. They would rather give up something themselves than hurt others to get what they want. As you develop your rational capacities, you become less controlling and less subject to the control of others.

See pages 28-31 for helpful diagrams.

Be on the lookout for...

...dominating behavior—yours and others'. Notice when people use language to dominate and control others. Detect differences between what they say and what they mean. Study your behavior to determine when and whom you tend to dominate. Are you "successful?" Is it worth it? Do you know anyone who routinely dominates people? Of course, there are circumstances when it is essential for one person to be in control, and when that person does so *reasonably* (as with the captain of a ship or a parent supervising a young child). Top-dog behavior, on the other hand, is designed to exercise power over others to serve one's interest or get what one wants.

Strategies for becoming less dominating:

- Identify areas in your life in which you irrationally try to control others. At home? At work? With your spouse? Your partner? Your children?
- Now consider the consequences. Are you really "successful" in getting what you want? To what extent does it lead to fulfillment? To what extent does it lead to frustration? Is it worth it?
- Notice how people "rationalize" dominating others. Note the reasons they give. Look for the actual reasons. Observe the usual results of domination in different situations.

- Legal, economic, and military domination are common in human history and are always seen by dominators as justified and essential. Develop your awareness of individuals and groups who invest energy and resources in controlling others. Notice how often "dominating" behavior is justified as "self-defense" or "in the interest of the person/group being dominated."

- Recognize that if you can't identify any part of your life in which you inappropriately control others, you are either highly self-deceived or you tend toward submissiveness when ego-centrically seeking what you want. See Day Nineteen, "Don't Dominate Others: Don't Be a Top Dog": Egocentric domination and submission are two sides of the same coin.

Don't Be Submissive; Don't Be an Underdog

A person playing a submissive role acquiesces to the domination of another or others to get something he or she egocentrically values—such as a sense of security, a feeling of protection, or a chance for advancement. These people exchange their freedom to achieve these ends (real or imagined). The submissive person, or "underdog," learns the art of helplessness. Characteristics typically include servility, or subservience, often accompanied by feelings of inferiority, inadequacy, and resentment. The underdog gains some indirect influence over the top dog through flattering subservience. Ironically, clever underdogs sometimes "control" unskillful top dogs. Submitters, like dominators, can be either successful or unsuccessful in achieving their goals.

> "Conformity is the jailer of freedom and the enemy of growth."
> —John F. Kennedy

People are often subservient in some situations and dominating in others. In other words, they switch roles in different situations. For example, they might be subservient at the office and dominating at home, or subservient to their spouse while dominating their children. At other times, they might be rational.

Top-dog/underdog (dominating/submissive) patterns are played out in numerous settings and situations in human life, and they lead to much cruelty and suffering. Reasonable persons avoid playing either of these roles. They recognize top-dog and underdog patterns in themselves, insofar as they exist, and they work to avoid them. They realize these tendencies will come up again and again in their thoughts, and therefore their behavior.

Going along with a decision when you disagree with it is not necessarily egocentric submissive (or underdog) behavior. For example, if another person knows more about a situation or issue than you, and you are not in a position to research the information yourself, it might make sense to go along (even though the little information you have about the situation might lead you to disagree). You have to decide, in any given situation and at any given moment, whether you are egocentrically submitting to others or whether you are rationally conceding. Self-deception is always a lurking force in the human mind. Dominating and submissive egocentric thought is always camouflaged, at least to some extent, through self-deception. Hence, it appears in the mind as logical.

To get command of your subservient nature, to the extent that you are prone to this tendency, begin observing your behavior closely when you are with others. Do you tend to go along with them without thinking through whether it makes sense to do so? Do you resent doing so afterwards? Do you feel like someone else has control over you? Only by bringing your subservient thinking and behavior to the forefront of your thoughts will you be able to get command of it and change it. If you have a strong submissive tendency, be prepared for a long, hard fight with it.

See pages 28-31 for helpful diagrams.

Be on the lookout for…

…submissive behavior—yours and others'. One of the hallmarks of submissiveness is conformity, a phenomenon common in human life. So look closely at your behavior in situations where you tend to conform. People who are submissive to others often feel resentment. Notice when you are resentful after having "gone along." When you submit against your will, do you notice yourself doing so, do you feel impotent, or do you just think negative thoughts? Perhaps you make a flippant or sarcastic comment. Perhaps you act in a passive/aggressive way. Don't blame others for controlling you; instead, realize you are allowing them to do so and figure out how to stop being submissive. Also notice when others are submissive in relationship to you. Can you determine what they are after? Do they get what they want through their submissive behavior?

Strategies for avoiding irrational submission:

- Pinpoint underdog behavior in yourself by identifying situations in which you tend to go along with others without good reason. In these situations, you might resent the subservient role you play. Yet your resentment is submerged. You don't explicitly resist. You say what you are expected to say (but don't really mean). After going along, you blame others for your frustration.

  To what extent do you find yourself behaving in a subservient way in your everyday life? Why are you doing it? What are you getting for doing it? What do you think would happen if you spoke up and said what you really think? What do you think you would lose?

- Identify specific circumstances in the past in which you behaved in a submissive manner. Did you feel resentful? Defensive? Irritable? Intimidated?

- Much submissiveness in society goes unnoticed, and most people are egocentrically submissive in some areas of their lives. For example, most people do not recognize their submission to their peer group, to irrational cultural requirements and taboos, or to socially defined authorities (people with high social status) who might lead people to act against their interests. Determine how important it is to be your own person, to think for yourself, and to be in command of your life. Insisting you are free does not make you free. Freedom begins with recognizing the extent of your slavery and subservience to social conventions, rules, and ideology.

- Realize that the submitter, like the dominator, can be either successful or unsuccessful. To the extent that you egocentrically submit to others, how "successful" are you? Do you tend to get what you want through submission? What precisely are you getting? What price are you paying for the reward? To what extent are you being dishonest in the situation—either with yourself or others?

- Catch yourself being submissive, such as in a meeting or in a conversation. At that moment, speak up. Say, as rationally as possible, precisely what you think. Notice the sense of self you gain.

- Take a global look at your behavior to determine the extent to which you are dominating, submissive, or rational. In what areas of your life do you tend to dominate? In what areas do you tend to submit? In what areas are you rational? What percentage of the time are you dominating, submissive, or reasonable? Start observing yourself closely to take control of yourself. When you do, you might be surprised by the inner sense of integrity you gain.

Don't Be Brainwashed by the News Media

Every society and culture has a unique worldview. This worldview shapes what people see and how they see it. It shapes perceptions and beliefs. News media across the world reflect the worldview of their own culture. This is true both because those who work in national

> "All journalists are, by virtue of their handicraft, alarmists; this is their way of making themselves interesting."
> —Lord Riddell

news media share the same views as their readers and because they need to *sell* what people within the culture want to *buy*. They need to present the news in ways palatable and interesting to their audience (to increase their profits). In the book *The News About the News*, Downie and Kaiser present the problems as follows:

> "The national television networks have trimmed their reporting staffs and closed foreign reporting bureaus to cut their owners' costs. They have tried to attract viewers by diluting their expensive newscasts with lifestyle, celebrity, and entertainment features, and by filling their low-budget, high-profit, prime time 'newsmagazines' with sensational sex, crime, and court stories" (New York: Knopf, 2002), p.19.

Mainstream news coverage in any culture operates on the following (often unconscious) maxims:

- "This is how it appears to us from our point of view; therefore, this is the way it is."

127

- "These are the facts that support our way of looking at this; therefore, these are the most important facts."
- "These countries are friendly to us; therefore, these countries deserve praise."
- "These countries are unfriendly to us; therefore, these countries deserve criticism."
- "These are the stories most interesting or sensational to our readers; therefore, these are the most important stories in the news."

The truth of what is happening in the world is far more complicated than what appears true to people in any culture.

If you do not recognize bias in your nation's news; if you cannot detect ideology, slant, and spin; if you cannot recognize propaganda when exposed to it, you cannot reasonably determine what media messages have to be supplemented, counterbalanced, or thrown out entirely. These insights are crucial to becoming a critical consumer of the news media and developing skills of media analysis.

Be on the lookout for...

...*products* of the news media throughout the day. Study the newspaper carefully, noting how "friends" of one's country are presented positively, whereas its "enemies" are presented negatively. Notice the not-so-important articles on the front page versus the important articles buried within. Notice significant world problems that are ignored or played down while the sensational is highlighted. Imagine how you would rewrite news stories to broaden their perspectives or to present issues more fairly. Make critical reading of the news a habit, not a rare event. Notice how TV news programs oversimplify the complex. Note how they target whatever they can sensationalize, and how they tend to dwell on stories that will be considered sensational by their viewers (rather than focusing on what is significant or deep). Note how they create and feed social hysteria (often around sexuality and what is considered criminal behavior).

Strategies for seeing through the news media:

- Study alternative perspectives and worldviews, learning how to interpret events from multiple perspectives.

- Seek understanding and insight through multiple sources of thought and information, not simply those of the mass media.

- Learn how to identify the viewpoints embedded in news stories.

- Mentally rewrite (reconstruct) news stories through awareness of how they would be told from multiple perspectives.

- See news stories as one way of representing reality (as some blend of fact and interpretation).

- Assess news stories for their clarity, accuracy, relevance, depth, breadth, and significance.

- Notice contradictions and inconsistencies in the news (often in the same story).

- Notice the agenda and interests a story serves.

- Notice the facts covered and the facts ignored.

- Notice what is represented as fact that should be presented as debatable.

- Notice assumptions implicit in stories.

- Notice what is implied but not openly stated.

- Notice what implications are ignored and what are highlighted.

- Notice which points of view are systematically presented favorably and which unfavorably.

- Mentally correct stories that reflect bias toward the unusual, the dramatic, and the sensational by putting them into perspective or discounting them.

- Notice when social conventions and taboos are used, inappropriately, to define issues and problems as unethical.

Carefully Choose the Ideas You Take in from Television, Ads, Movies, and the Internet

Group norms are propagated through virtually every structure in society, including mainstream television programs, movies, ads, and online information. Most of what is on television is superficial. Most television shows aim to engage and amuse, not challenge the mind or educate. Every day we are bombarded with messages that insult our intelligence while seeking to manipulate or influence our psyche (through intentional, subliminal messages). The vast majority of television programs, movies, and ads attract us either by feeding simplistic emotional beliefs (which flatter our infantile mind), or by stimulating our primitive drives for sexual gratification and violent revenge, or both. And it is merely naiveté or self-deception to say that you are not influenced by the shows you watch. Further, many people spend hours a day surfing the Internet, watching videos, and visiting websites. Ideas you get from the Internet affect who you are. Some of what is there is worthy of your time; some is inaccurate, misleading, or even dangerous, if taken seriously. Remember that irrational people and groups can have tremendous influence through the Internet, often through social networking sites. Radical groups can recruit people to their narrow-minded views.

> "Why should people go out and pay to see bad films when they can stay at home and see bad television for nothing?"
> —Samuel Goldwyn

131

Carefully observe...

...your television/movie-watching/web surfing habits today. Note how much time you spend watching television. Realize that most television programs are aimed at the intellectual level of an eleven year old. Ask yourself what you might accomplish if you spent less time in front of the television. Ask yourself what you get in return for the time you spend watching television. Notice the types of programs you tend to choose. Think through the implications of what you watch. What "messages" are you routinely receiving? Begin to notice the nationalistic or ethnocentric messages you see on television, in movies, and through the Internet. What cultural norms are encouraged? What taboos are discouraged? What types of behavior are sensationalized? How many shows or videos include some form of violence? How many of these types of programs or videos do you tend to watch? Also, pay close attention to the advertisements you see about you. How are products pitched to you, the potential buyer? Think about what advertisers assume about buyers. Pledge not to buy anything you see advertised today unless you independently assess the purchase in advance. Identify and begin to read at least one article or book on how ads influence people. When researching Internet sites and pages, determine whether the source can be trusted. What is the mission of a given website? What goals are behind it? Is information distorted or skewed to serve a one-sided agenda? What information might you need to balance a given view?

Strategies for critiquing television shows, ads, movies, and Internet resources:

- Notice the television shows that focus on violence: the violence of the "bad guys" in harming "good guys" and the violence of the "good guys" in taking violent revenge on the "bad guys" for their violence (you get to watch it both ways). What do you think are some consequences of television violence?

- Notice how rarely the mass media portray reasonable people doing reasonable things to advance a more reasonable world.

For example, notice how often irrational behavior in "intimate" relationships is portrayed as perfectly normal and natural (I hate you and I love you! I hate you because I love you! If you don't love me, I'll kill you!).

- Seek alternative television channels that question the status quo, such as Free Speech TV.

- Log the time you spend watching television. How could you spend your time more productively? Are you reading books that develop your mind? Are you reading anything that questions the status quo?

- Carefully choose the movies you watch. Consider watching realistic and insightful independently produced or foreign movies, rather than superficial Hollywood movies.

- Log the amount of time you spend on the Internet surfing the web each day. Look at the quality of the messages you see on the websites you visit. Consider how you are influenced by your favorite websites.

- Monitor your buying habits. How often do you buy the "advertised" brand? What does this tell you about yourself?

- Note the use of sexually suggestive images in product advertisements. Ask yourself: Will I really be more sexy if I buy and use this product?

- Rent the movie *Supersize Me*. Compare the information you get about McDonald's food in the movie with the information provided in the multitude of McDonald's ads. Think critically about food advertisements you see in the media. Compare the information these ads give you with the information they leave out (what is in the food, the health consequences of eating the food, and so on).

Don't Be Bamboozled by Politicians

Politicians want us to believe they are deeply concerned about the welfare of the people and that their actions are determined by what best serves the people. In other words, politicians present themselves as statesmen, so don't buy it. President Lyndon Johnson said, "Money is the mother's milk of politics." If you read between the lines, you will see quite easily that in politics, money, not concern for the public interest, is usually where the action is, with big money protecting big money. Consider this example from the news:[11]

"To be a chemist you must study chemistry; to be a lawyer or physician you must study law or medicine; but to be a politician you need only to study your own interests."—Max O'Rell

> "The Bush administration announced Thursday it will demand significant changes to a major World Health Organization initiative to battle obesity, saying the plan is based on faulty scientific evidence and exceeds the U.N. body's mandate...The WHO plan, which outlines strategies nations can use to fight obesity, has been widely applauded by public health advocates but bitterly opposed by some food manufacturers and the sugar industry."

---

11. "The White House to Demand WHO Obesity Plan Changes," *Press Democrat*. Santa Rosa, CA, January 16, 2004.

Needless to say, food manufacturers and the sugar industry have a vested interest in avoiding the obesity issue, because they are primary contributors to it. In many cases such as this, big business rules politics even at the expense of public health. Of course, this is one of many examples of money driving political decisions. If politicians don't do what those who bankroll them want, their money supply is cut off. Their primary concern is getting re-elected (so they can have power and prestige). In politics, sound bites, catchphrases, glitzy images, and mass delivery are the mechanisms for manipulating the people. Of course, there are a few needles in the haystack—those few people running for election not bought and paid for by big money. But they aren't usually elected.

Critical thinkers are not manipulated by slick-talking politicians—they recognize how politics work. Examine your thinking about politicians. How gullible are you when it comes to believing what politicians say? How often do you compare what they say with what they do?

As you go through your day...

...think about distinguishing politicians from statesmen. Politicians are people who pursue power to advance their vested interests. Statesmen are people who genuinely seek what is in the public interest. They are willing to state unpopular views and stand up against powerful groups and vested interests.

Look out for questionable statements that politicians make. Look on the surface at what they say. Look beneath the surface at what they mean. Determine what is in their vested interest. Notice how often their behavior supports their own interest while appearing to serve the good of the people or country. Determine what they want you to believe and why. Notice how they oversimplify problems to manipulate people. Notice how they often assert "truths" that contradict reality (which they blatantly ignore). Notice how often people believe them nevertheless.

Strategies for seeing through politicians:

- Listen closely to what politicians say and identify how they manipulate the electorate (for example, use language that reinforces stereotypes or provokes unnecessary fear). Always ask, "What is the interest of big money here?" And, conversely, "What is in the public interest?" Note the dearth of politicians acting in the public interest.

- Notice how politicians usually reflect dominant belief systems and reigning ideologies within the culture. That is, note how they lack intellectual autonomy.

- Keep in mind the vested interest of politicians. This enables you to predict their behavior.

- Become a student of political history, reading broadly in alternative sources to identify repeating patterns in political behavior throughout the years. Which of these patterns are prevalent today?

- Notice the extent to which politicians are entrenched in superficial and simplistic views. Nuances and depth cannot be expressed in sound bites.

Don't Be a Blamer

Some people spend a lot of time finding fault in and blaming others. And it is natural for people to blame others for their shortcomings. It is unnatural for people to take full responsibility for their actions. For instance, it is common for people to routinely blame one

> "Never does the human soul appear so strong and noble as when it foregoes revenge, and dares to forgive an injury."
> —E.H. Chapin

another in marriage ("You did this!" "But you did that first!"). This tendency comes from, among other things, taking one another for granted. People also frequently blame their parents for their irrational behavior. The simple fact is that few people survive childhood without emotional scars. All parents make mistakes. Some make significant mistakes, leading to emotional scars for their children. As a developing thinker, take responsibility for who you are and who you are becoming. This involves recognizing emotional baggage and getting past it. Living in misery, blaming your parents, and seeing yourself as a victim leads to depression and resentment. You have a choice. By taking charge of your thinking (and thus your emotions and desires), you can become who you want to be. You can become the author of your life. You can focus on the significant things and let go of the blame game.

Be on the lookout for...

... any tendency you have to blame others. Look out for others blaming you. What is behind the blame game? Do you blame others before they can blame you? Is the issue significant enough to justify blame?

Is something going on under the surface of the relationship that is leading to unreasonable blame? If you routinely blame your spouse for minor peccadillos, try to catch yourself doing so every time. If you blame your parents for your emotional scars, ask yourself what you gain by doing so. Focus your energy on letting go of the emotional "damage" you think your parents did to you. The past is gone; the present and future remain. Whenever you catch yourself blaming others for your failings, remind yourself that you now can create who you are becoming. Live in the here and now. Re-create yourself. Only *you* stand in your way. Only *you* can stop (your) blaming as a way of life.

Strategies for taking charge of who you are:

- If you are in the habit of blaming your intimate partner for insignificant things, ask yourself why. What is causing this negativity? Is the relationship in trouble? Are the two of you growing apart? Are you, at this point in your lives, incompatible? Face what is truly happening. Facing the truth is always best.

- Catch yourself "blaming" another person for something you are in fact doing, but the other person is not doing. For instance, if you have accused your wife of having an extramarital affair, are you really the one having the affair? Closely examine what is actually going on in your thinking. Don't let yourself off the hook.

- If you really think you have something significant to blame your parents for, write down exactly what that is and what the damage was to your emotional well-being. Make sure you distinguish between *fact* and *belief*. Belief can produce a self-fulfilling prophecy. Believing you have been harmed can result in harm. For example, believing that your parents destroyed your chance to pursue higher education, you might fail to pursue it—to get revenge on them.

- After you have compiled your list, read it carefully. Then ask yourself what you hope to gain by dwelling on any of these negative memories. Do you, as an adult, need to live in the past, as if you were still a child, unable to control your situation? Have you become a slave to unpleasant memories? Why not instead focus on what you can control, on opportunities, on what you can do?

- Take every moment you typically use to blame others, and transform your energy into action that leads to potential success and therefore positive emotions. For example, what can you learn from the mistakes your parents made? What can you do to be different, wiser, more just, and more compassionate than your parents were? What can you do to hold yourself responsible for your own decisions and actions?

- Make a list of all the sacrifices your parents made for you, and all the many everyday things they did for you. Then ask yourself whether you have given them sufficient credit for their good deeds. Many parents deserve far more credit than they get from their children, despite the mistakes they make. When you visit your parents or talk to them on the phone, don't dwell on the past. If necessary, think of your parents as people you have just met. View them as they are now. If your parents are still engaging in the behavior you perceive as harmful to you, perhaps you need to keep your distance from them. Perhaps you need to live away from them. Either way, act positively.

- Make a list of all the many things your intimate partner does for you or has given you. Vow to work through issues reasonably rather than blame one another. Again, if your partner routinely blames you for small mistakes and peccadillos, consider whether the relationship is healthy for you.

Consider the wisdom in this ancient Hawaiian proverb: "Either you eat life or life eats you." Only you can determine which of these two possibilities you embrace.

Don't Be Righteous: Show Mercy

Most of us think that if other people were to think just like us, the world would be a better place. Remember that we naturally believe that what we think is right. And when people don't think

> "We hand folks over to God's mercy, and show none ourselves."
> —George Eliot

like us and don't behave like us, we are often intolerant. We often want to see people punished for being different (though, of course, we wouldn't admit this). For example, more and more behaviors are criminalized in the U.S. because of intolerance for others' lifestyles. Consider prostitution. Many people find it *disgusting* and *perverted*. They therefore want prostitutes punished (for their *repulsive* behavior). Similarly, many people are upset by the idea of recreational drug use. They see people who engage in recreational drugs as social menaces. They feel a sense of righteousness when drug users are locked up (even though they themselves might drink alcohol, smoke cigarettes, or use mind-altering prescription drugs). Because there are now more people in jail in the U.S. per capita than in any other country in the world does not bother them. *Throw away the key* is their method! *Show no mercy*, their watchword! *Make them suffer*, their clarion call! Compassion, tolerance, and understanding are rare commodities. Though most people are compassionate toward their own family and close friends, few demonstrate compassion and tolerance toward those who think and act differently from themselves.

Be on the lookout for...

...opportunities to show mercy to others, and to display understanding, compassion, and forgiveness. Imagine a world in which doing so were routine.

Notice the extent to which others around you favor punishment and suffering as the proper response to "deviant" behavior. Notice the extent to which you do. As you read the newspaper, notice that severe sentences often are meted out for "crimes" that injure no one except the perpetrator.

Ask yourself how often punishment is extreme (in causing human suffering). Consider "three-strikes-and-you're-out" legislation. Consider the practice of trying children as adults. Consider "adult crime, adult time" legislation (laws aimed at giving adult-length sentences to children convicted of serious crimes). Also familiarize yourself with the approach of other countries (for example, Finland) that successfully return criminals to socially meaningful lives as soon as possible, with a low rate of repeat offenders. Think of ways to deal with cultural deviance without extreme punishment and social vengeance.

Strategies for showing compassion and mercy:

- Whenever you think someone should be punished for his or her actions, stop and ask yourself whether the greater good might not be better served in some other way. For example, would it not be better, in many cases, to think rehabilitation rather than prison?

- Whenever you think you are absolutely right and you judge another person's behavior to be intolerable, ask yourself: "What reasons do I have to support my view? How do I know I'm right? Could I be wrong? Am I being intolerant?"

- Study the situations that you find yourself most lacking in mercy, forgiveness, and understanding. In what situations do you think people should be punished rather than helped? On what reasoning do you base your conclusions?

- Consider the influence of social conditioning on your ability to see things from multiple perspectives. To what extent does your culture encourage or discourage forgiveness and mercy? To what extent does your culture encourage revenge upon, and condemnation and punishment of, the "wicked"? To what extent have you uncritically accepted righteous and merciless views encouraged by your culture?

Vow to Spend
No Time Worrying

Many people go through life worrying about problems rather than actively working to solve them. Sometimes they obsess about problems they can do nothing about. Consider the wisdom in this simple Mother Goose rhyme:

> For every problem under the sun,
> there is a solution or there is none.
> If there be one, seek till you find it.
> If there be none, never mind it.

It is remarkable how seldom people follow this sage advice. When faced with a problem, do your best thinking to see if you can find a solution. Open your mind to alternative possibilities. If you determine that you cannot solve the problem, let it go. Worrying and obsessing about something out of your control is emotionally painful and fruitless. Realize that, to the extent that you worry, instead of actively looking for solutions, your mind is failing you. Force your reflective mind into action. Identify the real options and determine the best one. Focus your energy on pursuing it. If there is nothing you can do in the situation, let it go; turn your mind to something productive.

> "Worry is interest paid on trouble before it becomes due."
> —W.R. Inge

Be on the lookout for...

... when you worry about problems rather than taking action to solve them. Notice when you worry while presenting a calm, unruffled exterior. Notice the negative emotions you experience when you worry. Notice when others worry, fail to act (when they can), and instead waste energy emoting about a problem. When you begin to worry, apply the Mother Goose rhyme to the situation. Act to solve problems (when you can). Let them go if you can't.

Worrying never adds to, but instead diminishes, the quality of your life.

Strategies for relinquishing the worrying habit:

- For every problem you have difficulty handling, follow Mother Goose. Ask yourself:
  - What precisely is the problem?
  - What are my options? Is there a possible solution under my control? Have I exhausted all possibilities for a solution? Have I considered every option available to me?
  - If this is a problem I cannot solve, or if I have exhausted all realistic options, am I letting go of the problem? Or am I still worrying about it? If so, why?
- Make a list of all the problems you worry about. Then go through the preceding steps for each one.
- Make a list of all the problems you have ever worried about and the results of those worries. To what extent did worrying help solve the problems? What were some consequences of your worrying? Which of these problems could you have solved through good thinking?
- Be proactive whenever you can. When faced with a troubling situation, don't allow your energy to be sapped by fretful worrying and obsessing. Instead, take action whenever you can, and to whatever extent you can. Use your energy productively, rather than destructively.

- Suppose you have done your best thinking about a problem but nevertheless have been unable to solve it. Notice your mind beginning to worry. At that point, immediately intervene with productive thinking. Remind yourself of the Mother Goose rhyme. Rethink the situation. Dig up new relevant information you previously missed, if possible. Keep concentrated on action. Be a doer, not a worry wart.

Be a Citizen of the World

In most countries, people are socialized to think in terms that advance the interests of their country—to be, in a word, "nationalists": "We are the best. We are number one. We stand for justice, truth, and freedom. When countries disagree with us, they are wrong. If they actively oppose us, they are our enemies. We sometimes make mistakes, but we always mean well. Those who oppose us usually have irrational, or even evil, motives.

"If patriotism is 'the last refuge of a scoundrel,' it is not merely because evil deeds may be performed in the name of patriotism...but because patriotic fervor can obliterate moral disvtinctions altogether."
—Ralph Barton Perry

They are jealous of us." This pathological way of thinking, when centered in a culture, is called "ethnocentrism" or "sociocentrism." It is universal and decidedly destructive. In his book *Folkways*,[12] W.G. Sumner puts the problem of ethnocentricity as follows:

> "Every group of any kind whatsoever demands that each of its members shall help defend group interests. The group force is also employed to enforce the obligations of devotion to group interests. It follows that judgments are precluded and criticism silenced.... The patriotic bias is a recognized perversion of thought and judgment against which our education should guard us" (p. 15).

---

12. *Folkways*, by W.G. Sumner, Salem, N.H., Ayer Company Publishers (1992) (originally published in 1906).

If we are to create a world that advances justice for the vast majority of people across the globe, we must become *citizens of the world*. We must denounce nationalism[13] and ethnocentrism. We must think within a global, rather than national, view. We must take a long-term view. We must begin to relegate the interests of any given country, including our own, to that of one of many: no more worthy, no more needy, no more deserving of the world's resources than anyone else on the planet. We must see the lives of people in other countries as no less precious than the lives of people in our own country. We must oppose the pursuit of narrow selfish or group interests. Integrity and justice must become more important to us than national advantage and power.

It is becoming increasingly clear...

...that the survival and well-being of humans depends largely on our ability to work together successfully and productively, to reach out to one another, to help one another. Yet, problems of nationalism and ethnocentrism are pervasive across the world. People are raised to see their country, or their group, as better than other countries or groups. They tend to favor the groups to which they belong. This is a natural tendency of the human mind. And it is a tendency fostered within most, if not all, cultures. By doing just a little research (for example, reading the newspaper, watching the news, reading traditional history books about your country), you can easily notice how often people present their country as the best country in the world. Notice how they whitewash their country's motives, representing them in glowing ethical terms (We are just! We are fair! We are good!). Notice how the national press fosters this image. Think of what you were taught in school about your country. Think about which parts of your country's history were ignored or distorted. Think about how your government describes its foreign policies (professing to care about other countries

---

13. Defined by Webster's New World Dictionary as militant, unreasoning, and boastful devotion to one's country or culture; excessive, narrow, or jingoist patriotism.

while its true motive is often to maintain a certain image or pursue some selfish goal).

Strategies for becoming a citizen of the world:

- Question the motives and actions of all governments. Recognize the similarity of politicians in all countries. Recognize the similarity of news media—serving vested interests—in all countries. Do not be taken in by emotional appeals. Base your decisions on universal values, not national interests. Support the development of altruistic international groups unconnected to vested interests.

- Imagine yourself to be a *citizen of the world*. Place world needs ahead of national agendas. Study problems from a global and historical point of view. Notice how the world and countries are stratified—with the "rules of the game" favoring the few, the powerful, and the wealthy, and with many other people being oppressed by the few.

- Notice the evolution of your views as you learn to think within a global perspective.

- Take one world problem—for instance, global warming, malnutrition, disease, and overpopulation—and find out as much as you can from multiple international sources. Then compare what your nation is doing about the problem. Are you surprised by what you find?

Do Something, Anything, to Help Make the World Better

You need only look around you to see problems in the world, problems caused largely by humans. The goal of critical thought is to improve how we think and how we act both in our personal lives and in relationship to others. As such, insofar as you are a critical thinker, you want to improve the quality of life on Earth. When you think critically, there are implications for how you treat and relate to others. You can contribute to a more just and sane world in many ways. From an ethical viewpoint, each of us is obligated to help others who are incapable of helping themselves. Each of us is ethically charged with doing *what we can* to improve the quality of life, both of humans and of other creatures susceptible to pain and suffering.

> "You will find that the mere resolve not to be useless, and the honest desire to help other people, will, in the quickest and delicatest ways, improve yourself."—Ruskin

Be on the lookout for...

...opportunities to improve the quality of life on Earth. Make a list of all the things you do currently to contribute to others' lives, or to the health of the Earth. Notice what others around you do. Do those around you contribute to a more just world, or do they mainly serve themselves? Make a list of some additional things you can do. Think about how you can fit into your schedule or your life some new ways of contributing. If you don't have a lot of time to spare, think about making greater financial contributions—but do something.

Strategies for contributing to a more just world:

- Carefully select a group that is organized to contribute to a better world. Many groups fight for justice in the world, for improved conditions, and for the alleviation of pain and suffering. Choose from local, national, and international groups. Select one and get involved—even if this means only sending money.

- Think about your circle of influence and act, using that influence to help others. For example, can you improve the quality of life for the people you work with? What about the people you live with? Work to create environments, wherever you can, where people help people. Notice how much you give to others and how much you take or demand for yourself.

- Discover your strengths, and use those strengths to contribute in any way you can. If you are good at writing, you might write letters to newspaper editors. If you have other special talents, use them to contribute to a better world. Everything, however little, counts.

- Most important of all, read widely and critically well-researched books on a range of world problems. You might be surprised to see how many world problems exist precisely because greed, selfishness, and vested interests dominate world resources.

- Work toward improving the lives of sentient (feeling) creatures. Notice how often people exploit these animals to serve their interests. Look into how cattle and "livestock" are treated by people in your culture. Research the living conditions of these animals. Go in with your eyes wide open. Let your interpretations and inferences be guided by the truth, not what you want to believe.

See Your Development Occurring in Stages

Some people think of critical thinking in this way: You are either a critical thinker or you're not. But this perspective is misleading. Remember, all of us think critically to some extent; all of us sometimes fail to do so. The quality of our thinking occurs along a continuum; each of us thinks at a higher level of quality in some dimensions of our lives than in others. We are all a mixture of critical and uncritical thought. Your goal should be to advance along the continuum, slowly but surely. The more seriously you take your thinking, the further and faster along the continuum you go.

> "Life is like playing a violin in public and learning the instrument as one goes along."
> —Samuel Butler

We can look at this continuum in terms of stages, from a vantage point that enables us to seek markers along the way, to look for rungs for lifting ourselves up to the next level. The following figure offers a visual snapshot of the stages of critical thinking development as we conceptualize them.

In stage one, unreflective thinkers are unaware of their thought as something that needs directing. They think, and then act on their thinking with very little sense that their thinking might cause problems. They are unaware that thinking is often flawed and hence requires tools for intervention. It seems that most people live the whole of their lives as largely unreflective thinkers.

Stages of Critical Thinking Development

Accomplished Thinker
(Intellectual skills
and virtues have
become second
nature in our lives.)

Advanced Thinker
(We are committed to lifelong
practice and are beginning to
internalize intellectual virtues.)

Practicing Thinker
(We regularly practice and
advance accordingly.)

Beginning Thinker
(We try to improve but
without regular practice.)

Challenged Thinker
(We are faced with significant
problems in our thinking.)

Unreflective Thinker
(We are unaware of significant
problems in our thinking.)

People reach stage two, the challenged thinker stage, when they are somehow introduced to a substantive idea of critical thinking, or are faced with the unsettling notion that there might be problems in their thinking. At this stage, people are beginning to open their minds to the possibility of a better way of living, but they aren't sure how to take the first steps.

We move to the third stage, beginning thinker, when we take up the challenge and start to explicitly examine our thinking for problems, however imperfectly. Because we lack intellectual discipline at this point in our development, our improvement is unpredictable. We are beginning to internalize some important critical thinking concepts and principles, but we understand them only at a novice level, or superficially. We realize at this point that we have a long way to go in our development.

People reach the practicing thinker stage when they create and follow through on a plan for their development, like reading this book and practicing using the ideas in it over an extended period of time. At this point, people begin to see real payoffs in their lives. They are less vulnerable to other people. They need less validation from others to feel good about themselves. They are less controlling of others. They are systematically studying the pathologies of their own thought. And they are developing as ethical reasoners.

Advanced and accomplished thinkers are rare, because it takes many years of committed practice to reach these stages.[14] People at these stages are in command of their decisions and their life in ways unimagined by those at lower levels. They are self-fulfilled; they are living an ethical life; they are fairminded thinkers who embody intellectual virtues across the domains of their lives.

Recognize that the native tendency toward self-deception, ever lurking in the human mind, can at any time impede your growth as a thinker. Even people at advanced levels are often self-deceived, but the power of native mental pathologies diminish as people become more disciplined and more committed to living an examined life. In our work with tens of thousands of people, we have seen many people reach the beginning, or even practicing thinker, stage, only to revert to unreflective thinker in many parts of their lives.

---

14. For more on the stages of critical thinking development, see Critical Thinking: Tools for Taking Charge of Your Professional and Personal Life by Richard Paul and Linda Elder, 2002. Upper Saddle River, NJ: Pearson Education.

Rather than seeing critical thinking as relevant and important to all domains or parts of life, people tend to pick and choose their critical thinking. You might, for instance, quite skillfully use the tools of critical thinking in your profession, while failing to use them much at all in your intimate relationship(s). The stages of critical thinking development refer to how we reason across all the areas of our lives, not in one or a few.

Your goal should be to develop through these stages to the highest point possible. Begin today by asking yourself which of these stages best captures your thinking at this point in your life. Are you largely unreflective but beginning to see the challenge? Have you already taken up the challenge? Are you at the beginning thinker stage, starting to internalize and effectively use some critical thinking ideas? Are you at the practicing thinker stage, with an ongoing strategic, systematic plan for your development?

Be on the lookout for...

...self-deception to impede your development as a thinker, at any of the stages. Look for excuses (rationalizations) you give yourself for why you are not taking your thinking as seriously as you could. Look at the behavior of others to see what stage they seem to be in.

Strategies for moving through the stages:

- Take your development seriously. Learn as much as you can about each stage and envision yourself moving forward a little each day. Write out a plan for moving from beginning to practicing thinker stage.

- Understand the role of intellectual humility in the development of critical thinking in daily life. Without intellectual humility, you will assume you already know enough and that there are no significant problems in your thinking. Hence, there can be little advancement as a thinker.

- Whenever you decide you have arrived as a critical thinker, take yourself back to the previous stage, or down a rung in the continuum. Intellectual arrogance is one of the great enemies of criticality; it is likely to impede your growth in many subtle ways even when you are actively working against it.

- Keep an ongoing plan for practicing critical thinking that will be modified as your mind is cultivated over time.

- Figure out how to use this book as part of your plan for long-term development. Remember, we suggest that you focus on each idea for a week at a time rather than a day. By now you should see why. How many of the ideas in this book have you deeply internalized? How many are you using every day? How would your life be different if you took any given idea more seriously than you have been to this point?

Educate Yourself

Although many people complete many years of school, including undergraduate and graduate studies, few people are *truly educated* in the highest sense of the term. Why? It is because few people have *learned how to learn* meaningful ideas. They are not learners for life. Instead, they form belief systems and then defend their beliefs for the rest of their lives. There is little development in their views. They do not expand the horizons of their minds. To the extent that they do develop, they tend to do so in certain narrow or technical ways (such as learning skills for succeeding on the job, or learning skills needed for a hobby). They lack the intellectual skills and traits unique to an educated person.

"A human being is not, in any proper sense, a human being till he is educated."—H. Mann

In 1852, John Henry Newman gave a series of lectures on education,[15] which were later compiled and published in the book *The Idea of a University*. In it, he describes the impact a well-designed education has on the mind of the learner:

> "...the intellect, which has been disciplined to the perfection of its powers, which knows and thinks while it knows, which has learned to leaven the dense mass of facts and events with the elastic force of reason, such an intellect cannot be partial, cannot be exclusive, cannot be impetuous, cannot be at a loss, cannot but be patient, collected, and majestically calm, because

---

15. Newman, J. New York: Longman's, Green and Co, 1852; 1912.

it discerns the end in every beginning, the origin in every end... because it ever knows where it stands, and how its path lies from one point to another" (p. 138).

In this book, we have introduced a number of the skills and traits of the educated mind. We have laid out an array of places *to begin*. To learn at a deep level, you need to take an active approach to your learning, realizing that education occurs throughout your lifetime, not just during your school years, and then only through committed practice. You need to understand the process of lifelong learning and explicitly choose to engage in it.

Place the cultivation of your mind...

...at the heart of your personal values. Begin to develop a plan for lifelong self-development. Study your own behavior. Lay bare contradictions and inconsistencies. Study the behavior of others. Notice how often ignorance is broadcast as knowledge. Notice how often what is arbitrary is presented as universal. See through to the shallowness of celebrity and status. See through pomp and ceremony. Vow to learn something important every day by reading important books and articles. Recognize that deep learning of new ideas, continually integrated with ideas already internalized, is the key to the educated mind, and the key to living a rational life. Reflect on ideas of significance. Identify opportunities to be with people who are seeking to improve their minds. Create a library, which includes works by the world's best thinkers past and present (including dissenting thinkers). Make it your home.

Strategies for self-education:

- Read widely. Read something every day that opens your mind to new and important ideas. Focus especially on great literature and the works of great thinkers. Go beyond current-day writings. Read the ideas of great dissenters throughout history. For suggested readings, see the section near the end of this book titled "Reading Backwards."

- Become your own historian, sociologist, and economist. You cannot be educated without a broad historical, sociological, and economic perspective. Understanding what is actually happening in the world requires studying human behavior over time, examining patterns and their implications. It means reading alternative historical accounts that help offset the sociocentric accounts that dominate the worldview of most people the world over. It involves becoming aware of the arbitrary nature of (most) social norms and taboos. It requires distinguishing universal ethical principles from variable social rules and taboos. By gaining a broadly grounded worldview, you will be better able to critique international news and irrational social practices. You will increasingly become your own person.

- Acquire the principles of critical thinking, tools at the heart of intellectual discipline and development. For additional resources, visit the Foundation for Critical Thinking (www. criticalthinking.org).

Figure Out Where to Go from Here

You have now been introduced to twenty-nine simple but powerful ideas. If you are to continue to develop, however, you will need to decide where you will go from here. Many strategies can help improve the quality of your life. One thing is certain: If you don't take a next step, there will be no next step. Like a rubber band that has been stretched, you will return to your original habits; you will revert to patterns of action based on beliefs you have unconsciously absorbed (but did not mindfully choose).

> "The chief art of learning, as Locke has observed, is to attempt but little at a time."—Johnson

Remember that the mind is free only to the extent that it is in command of itself. That is, your mind controls you—your thoughts, your emotions, your desires, and your behavior. Do you control your mind? (See the diagrams on pages 26-27.) When you take command of your mind, you decide, using skills of rational thought, what ideas to accept and what to reject, and what ideas to take seriously and what to ignore. You recognize the mind's natural desire toward selfishness, and you intervene with fairminded thinking and behavior. You recognize the mind's natural tendency to be rigid and close-minded. You therefore intervene to open your mind to other ways of looking at things. You recognize the mind's natural tendency to go along with group ideology, and so you closely examine your own behavior in groups to identify when and where you tend to mindlessly conform.

You will be in command of your mind only to the extent that you develop and continually redevelop plans for further growth. Otherwise, the egocentric and sociocentric tendencies of your mind (as with all of us) will pull you back to your comfort zone. They will keep you trapped in the ideology and mental habits you have developed unconsciously, in ideas that need questioning. Realize that the only way you will be able to *accurately assess* the ideas that guide your behavior is through intellectual discipline and skills you develop in your mind through your mind, consciously and deliberately. So, develop your plan for moving forward. Develop it today; revisit it every day.

Focus your energy today on...

... designing the next phase of your self-development plan. Make a list of books you plan to read in the next few months. Figure out how you will continue to develop your critical thinking abilities from this point forward. Continue your daily journal. Seek and regularly read alternative sources of news and worldviews.

Remember our previous suggestion. Namely, after you work through the *30-day plan*, graduate yourself to a *30-week plan*, focusing on one idea per week, rather than one idea per day. If you do this, you will deepen your understanding of each idea. Every important idea has many connections to other important ideas. Powerful ideas are powerful in light of their important connections. Every week, shift your emphasis. Your insights will multiply.

The worst plan is no plan. It is an approach that leads to low-level functioning. Remember, the pressure to conform to mass views continues unabated all your life. The egocentric forces in you will always have some power over you. Your plan to become your own person should be driving you forward. Begin afresh each day. Every day is a chance for a new beginning. You alone are the key to your intellectual growth. Don't allow anything—or anyone—to deter you from this goal.

Strategies for taking the next steps toward development:

- Explore other critical thinking resources, including those in the book *Critical Thinking: Tools for Taking Charge of Your Professional and Personal Life*,[16] as well as the *Thinker's Guide Library*. (Visit www.criticalthinking.org to read about these guides, as well as other books and materials.)

- Commit yourself to learning and applying one new and important idea every day (or every week).

- Continue to explore the ideas in this book, keeping a log of your reflections.

- Set aside a certain time each day for self-development. Make sure it is a time of peace and quiet. Realize that if you aren't willing to designate time for your mind to grow, you aren't truly committed to your personal development.

- Attend the International Conference on Critical Thinking sponsored by the Foundation for Critical Thinking. (Visit www. criticalthinking.org for more information.)

---

16. Paul, R. and L. Elder. *Critical Thinking: Tools for Taking Charge of Your Professional and Personal Life*, Upper Saddle River, NJ: Pearson Education, 2002.

Reading Backwards

One of the most powerful ways to educate yourself, to open your mind to alternative ways of experiencing the world, and thus to counteract the influence of social conditioning and the mass media, is to *read backwards*—to read books

"If we encountered a man of rare intelligence we should ask him what books he read."
—Ralph Waldo Emerson

printed 10 years ago, 20 years ago, 50 years ago, 100 years ago, 200 years ago, 500 years ago, 1,000 years ago, even 2,000 years ago, and so on. This enables you to step outside the presuppositions and ideologies of the present day and develop an informed world perspective.

When you read only in the present, no matter how extensively, you are apt to absorb widely shared misconceptions taught and believed today as the truth. The following is a sampling of authors whose writings will enable you to rethink the present to reshape and expand your worldview:[17]

- **More than 2,000 years ago:** Plato (especially on Socrates), Aristotle, Aeschylus, and Aristophanes
- **1200s:** Thomas Aquinas and Dante
- **1300s:** Boccaccio and Chaucer
- **1400s:** Erasmus and Francis Bacon
- **1500s:** Machiavelli, Cellini, Cervantès, and Montaigne

---

17. We recognize that this list of authors represents a decidedly Western worldview. We therefore recommend, once you have grounded yourself in deeply insightful authors from the Western world, that you then read works by the great Eastern authors. Contact us at cct@criticalthinking.org for a reading list of insightful Eastern authors.

- **1600s:** John Milton, Pascal, John Dryden, John Locke, and Joseph Addison
- **1700s:** Thomas Paine, Thomas Jefferson, Adam Smith, Benjamin Franklin, Alexander Pope, Edmund Burke, Edward Gibbon, Samuel Johnson, Daniel Defoe, Goethe, Rousseau, and William Blake
- **1800s:** Jane Austen, George Elliot, Charles Dickens, Emile Zola, Balzac, Dostoyevsky, Sigmund Freud, Karl Marx, Charles Darwin, John Henry Newman, Leo Tolstoy, the Brontes, Frank Norris, Thomas Hardy, Emile Durkheim, Edmond Rostand, and Oscar Wilde
- **1900s to present:** Ambrose Bierce, Gustavus Myers, H.L. Mencken, William Graham Sumner, W.H. Auden, Bertolt Brecht, Joseph Conrad, Max Weber, Aldous Huxley, Franz Kafka, Sinclair Lewis, Henry James, George Bernard Shaw, Jean-Paul Sartre, Virginia Woolf, William Appleman Williams, Arnold Toynbee, C. Wright Mills, Albert Camus, Willa Cather, Bertrand Russell, Karl Mannheim, Thomas Mann, Albert Einstein, Simone De Beauvoir, Winston Churchill, William J. Lederer, Vance Packard, Eric Hoffer, Erving Goffman, Philip Agee, John Steinbeck, Ludwig Wittgenstein, William Faulkner, Talcott Parsons, Jean Piaget, Lester Thurow, Robert Reich, Robert Heilbroner, Noam Chomsky, Jacques Barzun, Ralph Nader, Margaret Mead, Bronislaw Malinowski, Karl Popper, Robert Merton, Peter Berger, Milton Friedman, J. Bronowski, Peter Singer, Jane Goodall, and Howard Zinn

When you read backwards, you will come to understand some of the stereotypes and misconceptions of the present. You will develop a better sense of what is universal and what is relative, what is essential and what is arbitrary.

Recommended Readings to Augment the Strategies

The following readings come from three sources: *Critical Thinking: Tools for Taking Charge of Your Professional and Personal Life*, volumes of the *Thinker's Guide Library*, and the glossary in the back of this book. The book and *Thinker's Guide Library* (which includes an expanded glossary) can be found at the Foundation for Critical Thinking website at www.criticalthinking.org.

- **Day One, "Discover Your Ignorance":** See *intellectual humility* in the index of *Critical Thinking: Tools for Taking Charge of Your Professional and Personal Life*. See also *intellectual humility* in the glossary.

- **Day Two, "Strive to Be a Person of Integrity: Beware of Your Own Hypocrisy":** See *intellectual integrity* in *Critical Thinking: Tools for Taking Charge of Your Professional and Personal Life* and in the glossary.

- **Day Three, "Empathize with Others":** See *intellectual empathy* in *Critical Thinking: Tools for Taking Charge of Your Professional and Personal Life* and in the glossary. See also the *Thinker's Guide Library: Ethical Reasoning*.

- **Day Four, "Deliberately Target Your Purposes":** See *purpose* in *Critical Thinking: Tools for Taking Charge of Your Professional and Personal Life* and the glossary. See also the *Thinker's Guide Library: Analytic Thinking*.

- **Day Five, "Don't Be a Conformist: Think for Yourself":** See *intellectual autonomy* in *Critical Thinking: Tools for Taking Charge of Your Professional and Personal Life* and the glossary. See also *sociocentricity* in both references.

- **Day Six, "Clarify Your Thinking":** See *clarify/clarity* in *Critical Thinking: Tools for Taking Charge of Your Professional and Personal Life* and the glossary. See also the *intellectual standards* chapter in *Critical Thinking: Tools for Taking Charge of Your Professional and Personal Life.*

- **Day Seven, "Be Relevant: Stick to the Point":** See *relevance* in *Critical Thinking: Tools for Taking Charge of Your Professional and Personal Life* and the glossary. See also the *intellectual standards* chapter in *Critical Thinking: Tools for Taking Charge of Your Professional and Personal Life.*

- **Day Eight, "Be Reasonable":** See *reasonability* in *Critical Thinking: Tools for Taking Charge of Your Professional and Personal Life* and the glossary. See also the *Thinker's Guide Library: The Thinker's Guide to Intellectual Standards.*

- **Day Nine, "Ask Deep Questions":** See *questions* in *Critical Thinking: Tools for Taking Charge of Your Professional and Personal Life* and the glossary. See also the *Thinker's Guide Library: The Thinker's Guide to Asking Essential Questions.*

- **Day Ten, "Distinguish Among Questions of Fact, Preference, and Judgment":** See the *Critical Thinking: Tools for Taking Charge of Your Professional and Personal Life* chapter on questions.

- **Day Eleven, "Think Through Implications":** See *implications* in *Critical Thinking: Tools for Taking Charge of Your Professional and Personal Life* and the glossary. See also the *Thinker's Guide Library: The Thinker's Guide to Analytic Thinking.*

- **Day Twelve, "Distinguish Inferences from Assumptions":** See *information* and *inferences* in *Critical Thinking: Tools for Taking Charge of Your Professional and Personal Life* and the glossary.

- **Day Thirteen, "Don't Be Fooled by the Words People Use: Look Underneath Words to Unspoken Realities":** See *concepts* in *Critical Thinking: Tools for Taking Charge of Your Professional and Personal Life* and the glossary.

- **Day Fourteen, "When You Think You Have Arrived as a Critical Thinker, Think Again":** See the *Thinker's Guide Library: The Miniature Guide to the Human Mind*. See also *egocentricity* and the *stages of critical thinking development* in *Critical Thinking: Tools for Taking Charge of Your Professional and Personal Life* and the glossary.

- **Day Fifteen, "Be Fair, Not Selfish":** See *fairmindedness* in *Critical Thinking: Tools for Taking Charge of Your Professional and Personal Life* and the glossary. See also the *Thinker's Guide Library: The Miniature Guide to The Human Mind*.

- **Day Sixteen, "Get Control of Your Emotions":** See *feelings* and *emotions* in *Critical Thinking: Tools for Taking Charge of Your Professional and Personal Life* and the glossary. See also the *Thinker's Guide Library: The Miniature Guide to the Human Mind*.

- **Day Seventeen, "Take Control of Your Desires":** See *desires* in *Critical Thinking: Tools for Taking Charge of Your Professional and Personal Life* and the glossary. See also the *Thinker's Guide Library: The Miniature Guide to the Human Mind*.

- **Day Eighteen, "Don't Dominate Others: Don't Be a Top Dog":** See *egocentric domination* in *Critical Thinking: Tools for Taking Charge of Your Professional and Personal Life* and the glossary. See also the *Thinker's Guide Library: The Miniature Guide to the Human Mind*.

- **Day Nineteen, "Don't Be Submissive: Don't Be an Underdog":** See *egocentric submission* in *Critical Thinking: Tools for Taking Charge of Your Professional and Personal Life* and the glossary. See also the *Thinker's Guide Library: The Miniature Guide to the Human Mind*.

- **Day Twenty, "Don't Be Brainwashed by the News Media":** See *media bias* in *Critical Thinking: Tools for Taking Charge of Your Professional and Personal Life*. See also the *Thinker's Guide Library: The Thinker's Guide on How to Detect Media Bias and Propaganda*.

- **Day Twenty-One, "Carefully Choose the Ideas You Take in from Television, Ads, Movies, and the Internet":** See *media bias* in *Critical Thinking: Tools for Taking Charge of Your Professional and Personal Life*. See also the *Thinker's Guide Library: The Thinker's Guide on How to Detect Media Bias and Propaganda*.

- **Day Twenty-Two, "Don't Be Bamboozled by Politicians":** See the *Thinker's Guide Library: The Thinker's Guide to Ethical Reasoning*.

- **Day Twenty-Three, "Don't Be a Blamer":** See the chapter on *egocentricity* in *Critical Thinking: Tools for Taking Charge of Your Professional and Personal Life*.

- **Day Twenty-Four, "Don't Be Righteous: Show Mercy":** See the chapter on *egocentricity* in *Critical Thinking: Tools for Taking Charge of Your Professional and Personal Life*. See also the *Thinker's Guide Library: The Thinker's Guide to Ethical Reasoning*.

- **Day Twenty-Five, "Vow to Spend No Time Worrying":** See the chapter on *egocentricity* in *Critical Thinking: Tools for Taking Charge of Your Professional and Personal Life*.

- **Day Twenty-Six, "Be a Citizen of the World":** See *intellectual virtues* in *Critical Thinking: Tools for Taking Charge of Your Professional and Personal Life* and the glossary.

- **Day Twenty-Seven, "Do Something, Anything, to Help Make the World Better":** See the *Thinker's Guide Library: The Thinker's Guide to Ethical Reasoning*.

- **Day Twenty-Eight, "See Your Development Occurring in Stages":** See *stages of critical thinking development* in *Critical Thinking: Tools for Taking Charge of Your Professional and Personal Life* and the glossary.

- **Day Twenty-Nine, "Educate Yourself":** Visit www.criticalthinking.org for resources.

- **Day Thirty, "Figure Out Where to Go from Here":** Work through the chapters and *Test the Idea* activities in *Critical Thinking: Tools for Taking Charge of Your Professional and Personal Life*.

Glossary of Terms

The terms in this appendix come from our glossary of critical thinking concepts;[18] a close reading of the concepts can help you more deeply understand the concepts in this book. Note the interrelationships among the terms—look at these ideas as a web of concepts that, when deeply understood and integrated, can improve your life.

accurate: Free from errors, mistakes, or distortion. Accuracy is an essential intellectual standard and therefore an important goal in critical thinking. However, achieving it is often a matter of degree. The extent to which we have achieved it is determined by the conditions set forth by the question at hand and context (and how well we have met those conditions). Critical thinkers strive to accurately represent their own view and those of others. See *intellectual standards*.

assumption: A statement accepted or supposed as true without proof or demonstration; an unstated premise or belief; a belief taken for granted. By the word "assumption," we mean "whatever we take for granted as true" to figure out something else. Thus, if you infer that because a candidate is a Republican, he or she will support a balanced budget, you assume that all Republicans support a balanced budget. If you infer that foreign leaders presented in the news as "enemies" or "friends" of our country are in fact enemies or friends, you assume that the news is always accurate in its presentation of the character of foreign leaders. If you infer that someone who invites you to his or her

---

18. For the complete glossary, see Linda Elder's and Richard Paul's *A Glossary of Critical Thinking Terms and Concepts: The Critical Analytic Vocabulary of the English Language* (Tomales, CA: Foundation for Critical Thinking Press, 2009).

apartment after a party "to continue this interesting conversation" is really interested in you romantically, you assume that the only reason someone would invite you to his apartment late at night after a party is to pursue a romantic relationship. All human thought and experience is based on assumptions. Our thought must begin somewhere. We are typically unaware of what we assume and, therefore, rarely question our assumptions. Much of what is wrong in human thought can be found in the uncritical or unexamined assumptions that underlie it. For example, we often experience the world in such a way as to assume that we are observing things just as they are, as though we are seeing the world without the filter of a point of view. Skilled reasoners are clear about the assumptions they make, make assumptions that are reasonable and justifiable given the situation and evidence, make assumptions that are consistent with one other, and routinely seek to figure out what they are taking for granted in any given situation. Unskilled reasoners are often unclear about the assumptions they make, often make unjustified or unreasonable assumptions, make assumptions that are contradictory, and ignore their assumptions. See *inference* and *elements of reasoning*.

clarify/clarity: To make easier to understand; to free from confusion or ambiguity; to remove obscurities; elucidate, illuminate. "Clarity" is a fundamental intellectual standard and "clarification" a fundamental aim in critical thinking. People often do not see why it is important to write and speak clearly, why it is important to say what you mean and mean what you say. Two keys to clarification are the ability to precisely state and elaborate one's meaning and then to provide concrete, specific examples. See *accurate* and *intellectual standards*.

concept: An idea or thought, especially a generalized idea of a thing or class of things. Humans think within concepts or ideas. Concepts are intellectual constructs that enable us to identify, compare, and distinguish dimensions of our thinking and experience. Each academic discipline develops its own set of concepts or technical vocabulary to facilitate thinking within it. For example, "ethics" is dependent on a vocabulary of concepts. Thus, one cannot understand ethics without a clear understanding of concepts such as justice, fairness, kindness, cruelty, rights, and obligations. Every sport develops a vocabulary of concepts that enables those interested in understanding or mastering the game to make sense of it. We can never achieve command of our thoughts unless we achieve command over the concepts or ideas in which our thought is expressed. For example, most people value education, but relatively few people have a reasonable or developed concept of education. Few are clear about the differences among education, training, socialization, and indoctrination and thus confuse these very different ideas. Accordingly, for example, few are able to differentiate between when students are being indoctrinated and when they are being educated. This confusion is connected with the fact that few people can clearly articulate the skills, abilities, and intellectual traits of the "educated person." Critical thinkers distinguish the concepts implicit in educated uses of terms (as found in well-researched dictionaries) from the psychological associations connected with that concept in given social groups or cultures. The failure to develop this ability is a major cause of blind acceptance of social definitions, which often leads to social injustices. For example, because of its puritanical roots, many people in the U.S. have an underlying puritanical orientation to sexuality. They uncritically accept the largely arbitrary rules laid down by the culture (which dictate with whom people can have sexual experiences and under what conditions). They are, as it were, bound by society's conceptualization of sexuality. They don't recognize that there are many equally plausible ways to view sexuality. They fail to see "sexuality" as a concept at all; rather they see their view of sexuality, with all of its arbitrary cultural associations, as "the way things are and should be." For a richer understanding of this point, consult anthropological accounts of variations of "approved" and "forbidden" sexual practices in different societies throughout human history. Skilled reasoners are aware of the key concepts and ideas they and others use, are able to explain the basic implications of the key words and phrases they use, are able to distinguish special, nonstandard uses of words from standard uses, are aware of irrelevant concepts and ideas, use concepts and ideas in ways relevant to their functions, and think deeply about the concepts they use. Unskilled reasoners are unaware of the key concepts and ideas they and others use, cannot accurately explain basic implications of their key words and phrases, are not able to recognize when their use of a word or phrase departs from educated usage, use concepts in ways inappropriate to the subject or issue, and fail to think deeply about the concepts they use. See *elements of reasoning.*

confidence in reason: The deeply held belief that, in the long run, one's own higher interests and those of humankind are best served by giving the freest play to reason; confidence that encouraging people to come to their own conclusions through a process of developing their own rational faculties is the best path to the development of critical societies; faith that (with proper encouragement and cultivation) people can learn to think for themselves, form rational viewpoints, draw reasonable conclusions, think coherently and logically, persuade each other by reason, and become reasonable, despite the deep-seated obstacles in the native character of the human mind and in society. Confidence in reason is developed through experiences in which people reason their way to insights, solve problems through reason, use reason to persuade, and are persuaded by reason. Confidence in reason is undermined when people are expected to perform tasks without understanding why, to repeat statements without having verified or justified them, and to accept beliefs on the sole basis of authority or social pressure. See *intellectual virtues.*

critical: Given to judging, especially faultfinding, censorious; involving or exercising careful judgment or observation; nice, exact, punctual; occupied with or skillful in criticism; of the nature of, or constituting a crisis; involving suspense as to the issue; decisive, crucial, important, essential. There are several distinct uses of the term "critical" relevant to critical thinking and at least one use that is irrelevant. The irrelevant use is that which is overly given to faultfinding, without also being concerned with effectively dealing with these "faults." This use is connected with the term "cynic," or "pessimist," the person who habitually sees the negative aspects of life and is defeatist in view, and therefore rarely seeks solutions to problems. The uses of the term "critical" relevant to critical thinking are those focused on careful judgment and skillful critique, as well as that which is pressing, essential, and important. See *criticality, critical thinking,* and *critical person.*

critical person: One who has mastered a range of intellectual skills and abilities and embodies intellectual traits or virtues. When people use critical thinking skills largely to advance their selfish interests, they are critical thinkers only in a weak or qualified sense. If, on the other hand, they commonly use intellectual skills fairmindedly, routinely entering empathically into the points of view of others, they can be said to be critical thinkers in a strong sense. Of course, developing as critical persons is always a matter of degree, because no one could ever be the "ideal thinker." See *critical thinking, critical thinker, intellectual virtues, strong-sense critical thinkers,* and *weak-sense critical thinkers.*

critical society: A society that systematically cultivates critical thinking and hence systematically rewards reflective questioning, intellectual independence, and reasoned dissent. To conceptualize a critical society, one must imagine a society in which independent critical thought is embodied in the concrete day-to-day lives of individuals. William Graham Sumner, a distinguished anthropologist, explicitly formulated the ideal: "The critical habit of thought, if usual in a society, will pervade all its mores, because it is a way of taking up the problems of life. Men educated in it cannot be stampeded by stump orators and are never deceived by dithyrambic oratory. They are slow to believe. They can hold things as possible or probable in all degrees, without certainty and without pain. They can wait for evidence and weigh evidence, uninfluenced by the emphasis or confidence with which assertions are made on one side or the other. They can resist appeals to their dearest prejudices and all kinds of cajolery. Education in the critical faculty is the only education of which it can be truly said that it makes good citizens. (*Folkways*, 1906)"[19]

---

19. Sumner, W. (1940). *Folkways: a study of the sociological importance of usages, manners, customs, mores,* and morals. New York: Ginn and Co. (original work published in 1906).

Until critical habits of thought pervade our society (which will likely be decades, if not longer, into the future), there will be a tendency for schools as social institutions to transmit the prevailing world view more or less uncritically, to transmit it as reality, not as a picture of reality. Education for critical thinking requires that schools and classrooms become microcosms of a critical society. There are at present no existing critical societies on a broad scale. Critical societies develop only to the extent that the following conditions exist:

- Critical thinking is viewed as essential to living a reasonable and fairminded life.
- Critical thinking is routinely taught and consistently fostered.
- The problematics of thinking are an abiding concern.
- Closed-mindedness is systemically discouraged; open-mindedness is systematically encouraged.
- Intellectual integrity, intellectual humility, intellectual empathy, confidence in reason, and intellectual courage are everyday social values.
- Egocentric and sociocentric thinking are recognized as a bane in social life.
- Children are routinely taught that the rights and needs of others are equal to their own.
- A multi-cultural world view is fostered.
- People are encouraged to think for themselves and discouraged from uncritically accepting the thinking or behavior of others.
- People routinely study and diminish irrational thought.
- People internalize universal intellectual standards.

See intellectual virtues and strong-sense critical thinkers.

critical thinker: First see critical thinking. Critical thinkers are persons who consistently attempt to live rationally, fairmindedly, and self-reflectively. Critical thinkers are keenly aware of the potentially flawed nature of human thinking (when left unchecked). They strive to diminish the power of their egocentric and sociocentric tendencies.

They use the intellectual tools that critical thinking offers to analyze, assess, and improve thinking. They work diligently to develop intellectual virtues: intellectual integrity, intellectual humility, intellectual civility, intellectual empathy, and intellectual sense of justice and confidence in reason. They realize that no matter how skilled they are as thinkers, they can always improve their reasoning abilities. They recognize that they will at times fall prey to mistakes in reasoning, human irrationality, prejudices, biases, distortions, uncritically accepted social rules and taboos, and selfish and vested interests. They strive to contribute to a more rational, civilized society in whatever ways they can. They strive to consider the rights and needs of relevant others. The extent to which anyone can be properly described as a "critical thinker" depends on the skills, abilities, and traits of critical thinking the person exhibits on a daily basis. There is no "critical thinker" in the sense of "perfect" or "ideal" thinker, nor will there ever be. See *critical thinking, stages of critical thinking development, egocentrism,* and *sociocentrism.*

critical thinking: The most fundamental concept of critical thinking is simple and intuitive. All humans think. It is our nature to do so. But much of our thinking, left to itself, is biased, distorted, partial, uninformed, or down-right prejudiced. Unfortunately shoddy thinking is costly, both in money and in quality of life. Critical thinking begins, then, when we start thinking about our thinking with a view to improving it. Beyond this basic conceptualization, there are many ways to begin to explain critical thinking. Here are some examples:

- The art of analyzing and evaluating thinking with a view to improving it
- Disciplined, self-directed thinking, which meets appropriate intellectual standards within a particular mode or domain of thinking
- Thinking that commonly displays intellectual skills, abilities, and traits
- Thinking about your thinking while you are thinking in order to make your thinking better: more clear, more accurate, more reasonable, and so on

- Self-guided, self-disciplined thinking, which attempts to reason at the highest level of quality in a fairminded way

In understanding critical thinking, it is useful to recognize that it exists in many forms and manifestations. For example, much critical thinking is one-dimensional; some is global. Much critical thinking is sophistic; some is Socratic. Some is implicit; some is explicit. And finally, some is systematic and integrated; some episodic or atomistic. See *critical person, critical thinker, critical society, strong-sense critical thinkers,* and *weak-sense critical thinkers.*

criticality: Any of multiple forms of being skillful at criticism, such as in making judgments, evaluating literary or artistic work, assessing something with skill and ability, learning the art or principles of higher-order thought, or investigating scientific or scholarly texts or documents. The word "criticality" contrasts with "creativity." It accentuates the art of assessment or judgment and thus the state of being thorough, accurate, exact, or deep. It involves judiciousness, discernment, and the embodiment of intellectual criteria and standards. See *critical, critical thinking,* and *intellectual standards.*

defense mechanisms: A self-deceptive process used by the human mind to avoid dealing with socially unacceptable or painful ideas, beliefs, or situations. The human mind routinely engages in unconscious processes that are egocentrically motivated, and that strongly influence our behavior. When functioning egocentrically, we seek to get what we want. We see the world from a narrow self-serving perspective. Yet, we also see ourselves as driven by purely rational motives. We therefore disguise our egocentric motives. This disguise necessitates self-deception. Self-deception is achieved by means of defense mechanisms. Through the use of defense mechanisms, the mind can avoid conscious recognition of negative feelings such as guilt, pain, anxiety, and so on. The term "defense mechanisms" is used in Freudian psychoanalytic theory generally to mean psychological strategies used by the unconscious mind to cope with reality and to maintain a positive self-image. The theory of defense mechanisms is complex, with some theoreticians suggesting that defense mechanisms might at times be healthy (particularly in childhood). However, when these mechanisms operate in the mind of the normal adult, they pose significant barriers to rationality and the creation of critical societies. All humans engage in self-deception; however, critical thinkers consistently strive to act in good faith, to minimize their self-deceptive tendencies, to understand these tendencies, and work toward diminishing their frequency and power. Some of the most common defense mechanisms are denial, identification, projection, repression, rationalization, stereotyping, scapegoating, sublimation, and wishful thinking. See *denial* and *rationalization.*

denial: When a person refuses to believe indisputable evidence or facts in order to maintain a favorable self-image or favored set of beliefs. Denial is one of the most commonly used defense mechanisms. All humans sometimes deny what they cannot face—for example, some unpleasant truth about themselves or others. A basketball player, for example, might deny that there are any real flaws in his game in order to maintain an image of himself as highly skilled at basketball. A "patriot" might deny—in the face of clear-cut evidence—that his country ever violates human rights or acts unjustly. See *defense mechanisms.*

desire: A wishing, wanting, or craving for something. Desires, coupled with emotions or feelings, comprise the affective dimension of the human mind; the other dimension is cognition or thinking. Critical thinkers pursue desires that contribute to one's own pleasure or fulfillment (without violating the rights of others). Critical thinkers routinely examine their desires to make sure they are reasonable and consistent with one another. See *human mind, emotion,* and *thinking.*

egocentric domination: The egocentric tendency to seek what one wants through the unreasonable use of direct power over, or intimidation of, people (or other sentient creatures). Egocentric domination of others is overt or covert. On the one hand, dominating egocentrism can involve harsh, dictatorial, tyrannical, or bullying behavior (for example, a physically abusive spouse). On the other hand, it might involve subtle messages and behavior that imply the use of control or force if "necessary" (for example, a supervisor reminding a subordinate, by quiet innuendo, that his or her employment is contingent upon unquestioning obedience). Human irrational behavior is often some combination of dominating and submissive acts. In the "ideal" Fascist society, for example, everyone (except the dictator) is submissive to everyone above him and dominating to everyone below him. See *egocentric submission* and *egocentricity*.

egocentric submission: The irrational tendency to psychologically join and serve "powerful" people to get what one wants. Humans are naturally concerned with their interests and motivated to satisfy their desires. In a world of psychological power and influence, people generally learn to "succeed" in two ways: to psychologically conquer or intimidate (subtly or openly) those who stand in their way (through egocentric domination), or, alternatively, to psychologically join and serve more powerful others, who then: (1) give them a sense of personal importance, (2) protect them, and (3) share with them some of the benefits of their success. Irrational people use both techniques, although not to the same extent. When people submit to more powerful people, they engage in what can be termed "egocentric submission." Those who use overt force and control engage in what can be termed "egocentric domination." Both of these forms of behavior can be seen publicly, for example, in the relationship of rock stars or sport stars to their admiring followers. Most social groups have an internal "pecking order," with some playing the role of leader and most playing the role of follower. A fairminded, rational person seeks neither to dominate nor to blindly serve someone else who dominates. The opposite is *egocentric domination*. See also *egocentricity*.

egocentricity: A tendency to view everything in relationship to oneself, to confuse immediate perception (how things seem) with reality, to be self-centered, or to consider only oneself and one's own interests; selfishness; to distort "reality" in order to maintain a particular viewpoint or perception. One's desires, values, and beliefs (seeming to be self-evidently correct or superior to those of others) are often uncritically used as the unconscious norm for much judgment and "experience." Egocentricity is one of the fundamental impediments to critical thinking. As one learns to think critically in a strong sense, one learns to become more rational, and less egocentric. See *egocentric domination, egocentric submission, defense mechanisms, human nature, sociocentrism, unconscious thought,* and *strong-sense critical thinkers.*

elements of reasoning: The parts of thinking embedded or pre-supposed in all reasoning—purpose, question, information, inferences, assumptions, concepts, implications, point of view; also termed "parts of thinking," "elements of thought," and "structures of thought." All reasoning contains a universal set of elements, each of which can be monitored for possible problems. In other words, whenever we think, we think for a purpose within a point of view based on assumptions leading to implications and consequences. We use concepts, ideas, and theories to interpret data, facts, and experiences (information) in order to answer questions, solve problems, and resolve issues. Critical thinkers develop skills of identifying and assessing these elements in their thinking and in the thinking of others. Analyzing reasoning into its elements or structures represents one of the three sets of essential understandings in critical thinking; the other two focus on the assessment of thought (intellectual standards) and the development of intellectual virtues. See *purpose, question, information, inference, concept, assumption, implication, point of view, intellectual standards,* and *intellectual virtues.*

emotion: A feeling aroused to the point of awareness; often a strong feeling or state of excitement. Our emotions are integrally related to our thoughts and desires. These three mental structures—thoughts, feelings, and desires—are continually influencing one another in reciprocal ways. We experience negative feelings, for example, when we think things are not going well for us. Moreover, at any given moment, our thoughts, feelings, and desires are under the influence of either our rational faculties or our native irrational tendencies. When our thinking is irrational, or egocentric, irrational feeling states are actuated. When this happens, we are excited by (what is perhaps) infantile anger, fear, and jealousy, which can cause our objectivity and fairmindedness to decrease. Thus, emotions serve to signal whether things are working for us or against us. There is a range of emotional states regularly experienced by humans, from the highs to the lows—from excitement, joy, pleasure, satisfaction, to anger, defensiveness, depression, and so on. The same, or very similar, feeling state might be experienced in connection with rational or irrational thoughts and behavior. We might feel "satisfied," for example, when successfully dominating someone (see *egocentric domination*), or when successfully teaching a child to read. We might feel "angry" when someone refuses to follow our irrational orders, or when we perceive some injustice in the world. Therefore, the feeling of satisfaction or anger itself might tell us little or nothing about the quality of thought leading to the feeling. In any case, emotions or feelings are intimately connected with thoughts. For example, strong emotions can keep us from thinking rationally and might cause paralysis of thought and action. Because there is always a cognitive dimension to our emotions, having the ability to analyze the thinking that causes emotions is critical to living a rational life. Critical thinkers, for example, strive to recognize when dysfunctional thinking is leading to inappropriate or unproductive feeling states. They use their rational passions (for example, the passion to be fair) to reason themselves into feelings appropriate to the situation as it really is, rather than egocentrically reacting to distorted views of reality. Thus, emotions and feelings are not in themselves irrational; they are irrational only when they arise from and feed egocentric thoughts. Strong-sense critical thinkers are committed to living a life in which rational emotions predominate and egocentric feelings are minimized. See *human mind, intellectual virtues, irrational emotions,* and *strong-sense critical thinkers.*

emotional intelligence: Bringing intelligence to bear upon emotions; using skilled reasoning to take command of one's emotional life. The basic premise behind this idea is that high-quality reasoning in a given situation will lead to more satisfactory emotional states than low-quality reasoning. Taking command of one's emotional life is a key purpose of critical thinking. In recent years, the term "emotional intelligence" has been largely connected with a growing body of "brain" research in which attempts are made to connect brain chemistry to mental functioning, to connect, in other words, neurological processes that occur in the brain to cognitive/emotional processes in the mind. One must be careful not to overstep what can reasonably be inferred from this research. For example, some researchers have suggested that the amygdale (a so-called "primitive" part of the brain) can cause an emotional response to situations before the mind has had a chance to "think." This process has been blamed for things such as murder (for example, "he emotionally reacted and killed someone before his higher-order mental functions could stop him from doing it"). Yet, every emotional response is connected with some thinking of some kind, however primitive. If I jump in fear at a loud sound, I do so because I think something is potentially dangerous. Again the thinking might be primitive—it might be a split second—but it is thinking nevertheless. For the "average" person, taking command of one's emotional life does not require technical knowledge of brain chemistry and neurology. By studying the mind and its functions (such as thinking, feeling, and wanting), we have an abundance of knowledge we can use to develop emotional intelligence. For example, if we begin with the basic premise that emotions are always connected to some thinking, we can analyze the thinking that leads to our emotions, and the ways in which our emotions keep us from thinking rationally or reasonably in given situations. We can analyze the circumstances that lead to irrational thoughts and accompanying irrational emotions. See *emotions, human mind, rational emptions,* and *irrational emotions.*

ethical reasoning: Thinking through problems or issues that entail implications for harming or helping sentient creatures. Despite popular beliefs to the contrary, ethical reasoning is to be analyzed and assessed in the same way as any other domain of reasoning. Ethical reasoning entails the same elements as does all reasoning, and is to be assessed by the same standards of clarity, accuracy, precision, relevance, depth, breadth, logic, significance, and so on. Understanding ethical principles is as important to sound ethical reasoning as understanding principles of math and biology are to mathematical and biological reasoning. Ethical thinking, when reasonable, is ultimately driven by ethical concepts (for example, fairness) and principles (for example, "Like cases must be treated in a like manner"), as well as sound principles of critical thought. Ethical principles are guides for human conduct and imply what contributes to good or harm and what one is either obligated to do or obligated not to do. They also enable us to determine the ethical value of a behavior even when that behavior is not, strictly speaking, an obligation. Ethical questions, like questions in any domain of thought, can either imply a clear-cut answer or competing reasonable answers (matters requiring our best judgment). However, they are not matters of personal preference. It makes no sense to say, "Oh, you prefer to be fair. Well, I prefer to be unfair!" Ethics is often confused with other modes of thinking, such as social conventions, religion, and the law. When this happens, we allow ethics to be defined by cultural rules and taboos, religious ideologies, or legal statutes. For instance, if a religious group advocates killing the first-born male, or sacrificing teen girls to the gods, and religion is equated with ethics, then these practices would be seen as the right way to behave, or, in other words, ethically correct. Clearly this collapsing of ethics with any other system of thought has significant implications for the way we live, how we define right and wrong, what behaviors we punish, and what behaviors we advocate or "allow." See *intellectual standards.*

fairmindedness: A cultivated disposition of mind that enables the thinker to treat all perspectives relevant to an issue in an objective manner, without privileging one's own views, or the views of one's group. Fairmindedness implies being conscious of the need to treat all relevant viewpoints alike without reference to one's own feelings or selfish interests, or the feelings or selfish interests of one's friends, community, nation, or species. It implies adherence to intellectual standards without reference to one's own advantage or the advantage of one's group. There are three primary reasons why people lack this disposition: native egocentric thought, native sociocentric thought, and lack of intellectual skills necessary for reasoning through complex ethical issues. See *intellectual traits, intellectual standards, ethical reasoning, egocentricity,* and *sociocentricity.*

feeling: A particular emotional response; sometimes connected with physical sensations. Feelings or emotions are integrally connected with thoughts. Feelings influence thoughts. Thoughts influence feelings. The relationship is reciprocal. Thus, "I feel angry when I think I have been wronged." And "the more I think I have been wronged, the more angry I become." Critical thinkers use their thinking to take command of their feelings. See *emotion, human mind,* and *emotional intelligence.*

human nature: The common qualities, instincts, inherent tendencies, and capacities of human beings. People have both a primary and secondary nature. Our primary nature is spontaneous, egocentric, and subject to irrational belief formation. It is the basis for our instinctual thought. People need no training to believe what they want to believe: what serves their immediate interests, what preserves their sense of personal comfort and righteousness, what minimizes their sense of inconsistency, and what presupposes their own correctness. People need no special training to believe what those around them believe: what their parents and friends believe, what is taught to them by religious and school authorities, what is repeated often by the media, and what is commonly believed in their nation and culture. People need no training to think that those who disagree with them are wrong and probably prejudiced. People need no training to assume that their own most fundamental beliefs are self-evidently true or easily justified by evidence. People naturally and spontaneously identify with their own beliefs. They often experience disagreement as a personal attack. The resulting defensiveness interferes with their capacity to empathize with, or enter into, other points of view. On the other hand, people need extensive and systematic practice to develop their secondary nature and their implicit capacity to function as rational persons. They need extensive and systematic practice to recognize the tendencies they have to form irrational beliefs. They need extensive practice to develop a dislike of inconsistencies in their thought, a love of clarity, a passion to seek reasons and evidence, and to be fair to points of view other than their own. People need extensive practice to recognize that they live inferentially, that they do not have a direct pipeline to reality, and that it is perfectly possible to have an overwhelming inner sense of the correctness of one's views and still be wrong. See *egocentricity, sociocentricity, rational, rational self,* and *intellectual virtues.*

implication/imply: Claims or truths that follow from other claims or truths. They represent logical relationships between ideas or things. Imply means to indicate indirectly or by allusion; hint; suggest; intimate; entail; verbal implications are ideas, assumptions, viewpoints, beliefs, and so on. implied by the words used in speech or communication, given the logic of the language. By the "implications of reasoning," we mean that which follows from some dimension of thought. It means that to which our thinking is leading us. If you say to someone that you "love" him or her, you imply that you are concerned with the person's welfare. If you make a promise, you imply that you intend to keep it. If you call a country a "democracy," you imply that the political power is in the hands of the people at large (instead of a powerful minority). If you call yourself a feminist, you imply that you are in favor of political, social, and economic equality of women and men. We often test people's credibility by seeing whether they behave in accordance with what their words imply. "Say what you mean and mean what you say" is a sound principle of critical thinking (and of personal integrity). One of the most important skills of critical thinking is the ability to distinguish between what a statement or situation actually implies and what people might carelessly infer from that statement or situation. Critical thinkers try to monitor their inferences so as to infer no more or less than that which is actually implied in any given context. When speaking, critical thinkers try to use words that imply only what they can legitimately justify. They recognize that there are established word usages that generate established implications. Skilled reasoners clearly and precisely articulate the implications and possible consequences of their reasoning, search for potentially negative as well as potentially positive consequences, and anticipate the likelihood of unexpected negative and positive implications. Unskilled reasoners concentrate on few or none of the implications and consequences of holding a position or making a decision, are unclear and imprecise in the possible consequences they articulate, focus only the consequences they had in mind at the beginning of reasoning through an issue, either positive or negative, but usually not both, and are surprised when their decisions have unexpected consequences. See *elements of reasoning*.

infer/inference: A step of the mind, an act of the intellect, by which one concludes that something is so in light of something else being so, or seeming to be so; it suggests the arriving at a decision or opinion by reasoning from known facts or evidence. People continually make inferences; for every time we make sense of things, inferences are involved in that process. For example, if you come at me with a knife in your hand, I would probably infer that you mean to do me harm. Inferences might be logical or illogical, justifiable or unjustifiable. And even when they are illogical, or unjustifiable, they are generally viewed by the mind as "the right way to think." This is true because most people have difficulty separating inferences from the raw data of their experience. They don't recognize that they are continually making inferences. And they don't know that inferences are based not only on information, but on assumptions as well (that often lie at the unconscious level of thought). Critical thinkers take notice of their inferences, recognizing that whenever they make an inference, it may or may not be justified. They separate information from inferences. Skilled reasoners are clear about the inferences they make, clearly articulate their inferences, usually make inferences that follow from the evidence or reasons presented, often make inferences that are deep in thought rather than superficial, often make inferences or come to conclusions that are reasonable, make inferences or come to conclusions that are consistent with one another, and understand the assumptions that lead to inferences. Unskilled reasoners are often unclear about the inferences they make, do not clearly articulate their inferences, often make inferences that do not follow from the evidence or reasons presented, often make inferences that are superficial, often make inferences or come to conclusions that are unreasonable, often make inferences or come to conclusions that are contradictory, and do not seek to figure out the assumptions that lead to inferences. See *elements of reasoning, implication,* and *assumption.*

information: Statements, statistics, data, facts, diagrams gathered in any way, as by reading, observation, or hearsay. By "using information in our reasoning," we mean using some set of facts, data, or experiences to support our conclusions. Information itself does not imply validity or accuracy. Information used in reasoning can be accurate or inaccurate, relevant or irrelevant. It might be presented equitably, or in a manner that distorts its proper weight or value. Information is always interpreted in the light of one's assumptions. Often when someone is reasoning, it makes sense to ask, "Upon what facts or information are you basing your reasoning?" The informational basis for reasoning is always important and often crucial. For example, in deciding whether to support capital punishment, we need factual information. Information one might use in supporting the view that capital punishment is unjustified might include: "Since the death penalty was reinstated by the Supreme Court in 1976, for every seven prisoners who were executed, one prisoner awaiting execution was found to be innocent and released." "At least 381 homicide convictions have been overturned since 1963 because prosecutors concealed evidence of innocence or presented evidence they knew to be false." "A study by the U.S. General Accounting Office found racial prejudice in death sentencing. . . . Killers of whites were proportionally more likely to be executed than were killers of blacks." "Since 1984, 34 mentally retarded people have been executed." Skilled reasoners assert a claim only when they have sufficient evidence to back it up, can articulate and evaluate the information behind their claims, actively search for information against (not just for) their own position, focus on relevant information and disregard what is irrelevant to the question at issue, draw conclusions only to the extent that they are supported by the data and sound reasoning, and state their evidence clearly and fairly. Unskilled reasoners assert claims without considering all relevant information, do not articulate the information they are using in their reasoning and so do not subject it to rational scrutiny, gather information only when it supports their own point of view, do not carefully distinguish between relevant information and irrelevant information, make inferences that go beyond what the data support, and distort the data or state it inaccurately. See *element of reasoning, inferences,* and *assumptions.*

   intellect/intellectual/intelligent: The term "intellectual" often means requiring the intellect, or having or showing a high degree of intelligence. The term "intellect" implies the ability to reason or understand or to perceive relationships, differences, and so on. It refers to that part of the mind that knows or understands. It might also imply the power of thought, great mental ability, or a high degree of intelligence. The terms "intelligent" or "intelligence" imply having or showing an alert mind, bright, perceptive, informed, clever, and wise. They generally imply the ability to learn or understand from experience, the ability to acquire and retain knowledge, and the ability to respond quickly and successfully to new situations. They characteristically imply or presuppose use of the faculty of reason in solving problems, directing conduct successfully, and making sound judgments. Because skilled reasoning is at the heart of intelligent decision-making and the ability to make sound judgments, the development of the intellect presupposes critical thinking. It is through the concepts and principles of critical thinking, applied in context, that we develop our abilities to reason well. It might be argued that the cultivation of the intellect and the development of critical thinking skills, abilities, and traits are in essence one and the same thing. John Henry Newman, a distinguished nineteenth century scholar, richly detailed and exemplified the relationship between the cultivation of the intellect and the principles of critical thinking. Consider one short passage from his book: …"the intellect, which has been disciplined to the perfection of its powers, which knows, and thinks while it knows, which has learned to leaven the dense mass of facts and events with the elastic force of reason, such an intellect cannot be partial, cannot be exclusive, cannot be impetuous, cannot be at a loss…because it discerns the end in every beginning, the origin in every end, the law in every interruption, the limit in each delay; because it ever knows where it stands, and how its path lies from one point to another (p. 100)."[20] Certainly, some people are born with higher degrees of natural "intelligence." Still, raw intelligence needs development (through critical thought). And often the raw power of the intellect

---

20. Newman, J. Originally published in 1852, this reference is taken from *The Idea of a University* (1996), London: Yale University Press.

is used for ill, rather than for good. This results in weak sense critical thinking (such as skilled, but unethical thinking). Through the tools of critical thinking, we can actively cultivate the intellect; we can develop our intellectual capacities; and we can foster strong sense critical thinking (skilled and ethical thinking). See *strong-sense critical thinkers* and *weak-sense critical thinkers*.

intellectual arrogance: The natural egocentric human tendency to believe that we know more than we do, that our thinking is rarely wrong, that we don't need to improve our thinking, that we are in receipt of "the truth." One of the most powerful barriers to the development of human thought is the egocentric tendency to think that whatever we believe is true. Critical thinkers are keenly aware of this problem in human thought, and are on the lookout for it in their own thinking. They work to develop the intellectual virtue of intellectual humility; they are committed to diminishing the power and likelihood of intellectual arrogance in their thinking. But they recognize that they will always be, at times, subject to this tendency. See *intellectual humility* and *intellectual virtues*.

intellectual autonomy: Having independent, rational control of one's beliefs, values, assumptions, and inferences. The ideal of critical thinking is to learn to think for oneself, to gain command over one's thought processes. Intellectual autonomy does not entail willfulness, stubbornness, or rebellion. It entails a commitment to analyzing and evaluating beliefs on the basis of reason and evidence, to question when it is rational to question, to believe when it is rational to believe, and to agree when it is rational to agree. The opposite of intellectual autonomy is intellectual conformity. See *intellectual virtues*.

intellectual civility: A commitment to take others seriously as thinkers, to treat them as intellectual equals, to grant respect and full attention to their views—a commitment to persuade rather than browbeat. Intellectual civility is distinguished from intellectual rudeness: verbally attacking others, dismissing them, and stereotyping their views. Intellectual civility is not a matter of mere courtesy but, instead, arises from a sense that everyone has a right to have his or her views heard and to be treated politely in the process. The opposite of intellectual civility is intellectual rudeness. Theoreticians attempt to limit critical thinking to one or a few possible objects. For example, when critical thinking is based on formal logic, the focus of analysis and assessment is limited to arguments of a formal character. Other theoreticians might include problems and decisions, in addition to arguments as possible objects. Some equate critical thinking with the Scientific Method. In the most robust form of critical thinking, there are an unlimited number of possible intellectual constructs that can be analyzed and assessed, including: assumptions, concepts, theories, principles, purposes, questions, reports, speeches, plays, art, engineering plans, historical accounts, anthropological orientations, scientific theories, technical objects (created by human plans), ideologies, books, essays, poems, music, sports, cooking, and so on. See *intellectual virtues*.

intellectual courage: The willingness to face and fairly assess ideas, beliefs, or viewpoints to which we have strong negative reactions; the willingness to critically analyze beliefs we hold dear. Intellectual courage arises from the recognition that ideas considered dangerous or absurd are sometimes rationally justified (in whole or in part), and that conclusions or beliefs espoused by those around us, or inculcated in us, are sometimes false or misleading. To determine for ourselves which is which, we must not passively and uncritically "accept" what we have "learned." Intellectual courage comes into play here, because when we look at things objectively, we will inevitably come to see some truth in some ideas considered dangerous and absurd, and some distortion or falsity in some ideas strongly held in our social group. It takes courage to be true to our own thinking in such circumstances. Examining cherished beliefs is difficult, and the penalties for non-conformity are often severe, even in putative democracies. The opposite of intellectual courage is intellectual cowardice. See *intellectual virtues*.

intellectual curiosity: A strong desire to deeply understand, to figure things out, to propose and assess useful and plausible hypotheses and explanations; to learn, to find out; inquisitive. Humans are innately curious. This is exemplified by the fact that young children are often a veritable fountain of questions. However this native tendency is typically discouraged in present-day societies and schooling. People do not learn well and do not gain knowledge, unless they are motivated to do so. Schooling at all levels should encourage intellectual curiosity and should encourage students to question and think for themselves, and to figure things out using their thinking. Otherwise, the intellect becomes deadened, innate curiosity is diminished, and students lose the motivation to learn. The opposite of intellectual curiosity is intellectual apathy. See *intellectual virtues*.

intellectual discipline: The trait of thinking in accordance with intellectual standards, intellectual rigor, carefulness, thoroughness, and conscious control. Undisciplined thinkers do not recognize when they come to unwarranted conclusions, confuse ideas, fail to consider pertinent evidence, and so on. Intellectual discipline is at the heart of becoming a critical person. It takes discipline of mind to stay focused on the intellectual task at hand, to locate and carefully assess needed evidence, to systematically analyze and address questions and problems, and to hold one's thinking to intellectual standards such as clarity, precision, completeness, and consistency. Intellectual discipline is achieved slowly, progressively, and only through receptivity and commitment. See *intellectual virtues* and *intellectual standards*.

intellectual empathy: Understanding the need to imaginatively put oneself in the place of others to genuinely understand them. To develop intellectual empathy, we must recognize the natural human tendency to identify truth with our immediate perceptions or long-standing beliefs. Intellectual empathy correlates with the ability to accurately reconstruct the viewpoints and reasoning of others and to reason from premises, assumptions, and ideas other than our own. This trait also requires that we remember occasions when we were wrong, despite an intense conviction that we were right, and consider that we might be similarly deceived in a case at hand. The opposite of intellectual empathy is intellectual closemindedness. See *intellectual virtue* and *fairmindedness*.

intellectual engagement: Directing one's full attention to learning or understanding something. To learn deeply and insightfully requires engaging the intellect in the process of learning. Too often, intellectual engagement is missing from the teaching and learning process. When this happens, students are alienated from learning and content is learned superficially or temporarily. To engage the intellect is to understand how to learn deeply, to see the value in learning, and to have confidence in one's ability to figure things out for oneself. In its fullest sense, it entails the ability to connect powerful ideas within subjects and disciplines by living more rationally and reasonably.

intellectual humility: Awareness of the limits of one's knowledge, including sensitivity to circumstances in which one's native egocentrism is likely to function self-deceptively; sensitivity to bias and prejudice in, and limitations of, one's viewpoint. Intellectual humility is based on the recognition that people should not claim more than they actually know. It does not imply spinelessness or submissiveness. It implies the lack of intellectual pretentiousness, boastfulness, or conceit, combined with insight into the strengths or weaknesses of the logical foundations of one's beliefs. The opposite of intellectual humility is intellectual arrogance. See *intellectual virtues*.

intellectual integrity: Recognition of the need to be true to one's own thinking, to be consistent in the intellectual standards one applies, to hold oneself to the same rigorous standards of evidence and proof to which one holds one's antagonists, to practice what one advocates for others, and to honestly admit discrepancies and inconsistencies in one's own thought and action. This trait develops best in a supportive atmosphere in which people feel secure and free enough to honestly acknowledge their inconsistencies, and can develop and share realistic ways of ameliorating them. It requires honest acknowledgment of the difficulties of achieving greater consistency. The opposite of intellectual integrity is intellectual hypocrisy. See *intellectual virtues*.

intellectual perseverance: Willingness and consciousness of the need to pursue intellectual insights and truths despite difficulties, obstacles, and frustrations; firm adherence to rational principles despite irrational opposition of others; a sense of the need to struggle with confusion and unsettled questions over an extended period of time in order to achieve deeper understanding or insight. This trait is undermined when teachers and others continually provide students with "answers," rather than encouraging them to formulate questions on their own and pursue answers to the questions using their best reasoning. It is undermined when teachers substitute formulas, algorithms, and short cuts for careful, independent thought. It is undermined when memorization is substituted for deep learning. The opposite of intellectual perseverance is intellectual indolence or laziness. See *intellectual virtues*.

intellectual responsibility: A sense of obligation to fulfill one's duties in intellectual matters and to develop one's mind to the extent of one's capacities. Intellectually responsible people recognize that all humans are obligated to achieve a high level of soundness in their reasoning and are deeply committed to gathering adequate evidence for their beliefs. Intellectually responsible people are committed to developing their minds throughout their lives and to come increasingly closer to the rational ideal. See *intellectual virtues*.

intellectual sense of justice: Willingness and consciousness of the need to entertain all viewpoints sympathetically and to assess them without reference to one's own feelings or vested interests, or the feelings or vested interests of one's friends, community, or nation. Intellectual sense of justice is closely connected with *intellectual integrity* and *fairmindedness*. See also *intellectual virtues*.

intellectual standards: The standards or criteria necessary for reasoning at a high level of skill and for making sound judgments. Intellectual standards are necessary for forming knowledge (as against unsound beliefs), for understanding, and for thinking rationally and logically. Intellectual standards are fundamental to critical thinking. Some essential intellectual standards are clarity, accuracy, relevance, precision, breadth, depth, logicalness, significance, consistency, fairness, completeness, and reasonability. Intellectual standards are presupposed in every domain of human thought, and in every discipline and subject. To develop one's mind and discipline one's thinking using these standards requires regular practice and long-term cultivation. Of course, achieving these standards is a relative matter and varies to some degree among domains of thought. Being precise while doing mathematics is not the same as being precise while writing a poem, describing an experience, or explaining a historical event. We can roughly classify intellectual standards into two categories: "micro-intellectual standards" and "macro-intellectual standards." Micro-intellectual standards are those intellectual standards that pinpoint specific aspects of intellectual assessment—for example, is the thinking clear? Is the information relevant? Are the purposes consistent? Though essential to skilled reasoning, meeting one or more micro-standards does not necessarily fulfill the intellectual task at hand. This is true because thinking can be clear but not relevant; it can be relevant but not precise; it can be accurate but not sufficient, and so forth. When the reasoning we need to engage in is monological (that is, focused on a question with an established settlement procedure), micro-intellectual standards may suffice. But to reason well through multilogical issues (that is, problems or issues that require that we reason within conflicting points of view), we need not only micro-, but macro-intellectual standards as well. Macro-intellectual standards are broader in scope; they integrate our use of micro-standards; they expand our intellectual understandings. For example, when reasoning through a complex issue, we need our thinking to be reasonable or sound (satisfying, in other words, broad intellectual standards). For thinking to be reasonable or sound, it needs, at minimum, to be clear, accurate, and relevant. Moreover, when more than one viewpoint is relevant to an issue, we need to be able to compare, contrast, and integrate insights from relevant viewpoints before taking a position on the issue ourselves. Thus, the use of macro-intellectual standards (such as reasonability and soundness) help guide the reasoning toward depth, comprehensiveness, and integration of thought. See *accurate, clarify, logical, reasonableness,* and *relevant.*

intellectual traits/dispositions/virtues: The traits of mind and character necessary for correct action and thinking; the dispositions of mind and character essential for fairminded rationality; the virtues that distinguish the narrow-minded, self-serving critical thinker from the open-minded, truth-seeking critical thinker. Intellectual traits include, but are not limited to intellectual sense of justice, intellectual perseverance, intellectual integrity, intellectual humility, intellectual empathy, intellectual courage, intellectual curiosity, intellectual discipline, (intellectual) confidence in reason, and intellectual autonomy. The hallmark of the strong sense critical thinker is the embodiment of and deep commitment to these intellectual virtues. Yet, the extent to which anyone lives in accordance with them on a daily basis is a matter of degree, no actual person achieving that of the hypothetical ideal thinker. Intellectual traits are interdependent. Each is fully developed only in conjunction with the development of the others. They develop only through years of commitment and practice. They cannot be imposed from without; they must be cultivated by encouragement and example. See the intellectual traits listed previously.

irrational/irrationality: Lacking the power to reason; contrary to reason or logic; senseless, unreasonable, and absurd. Humans are both rational and irrational. We have innate egocentric and sociocentric tendencies that often lead us to do things that are illogical (though they seem to us at the time to be perfectly logical). We don't automatically sense what is reasonable in any given situation. Rather, the extent to which we think and act rationally depends on how well our rational capacities have been developed. It depends on the extent to which we have learned to go beyond our natural prejudices and biases, beyond our narrow, self-serving viewpoint, to see what makes most sense to do and believe in a given situation. Critical thinkers are alert to their irrational tendencies. They strive to become rational, fairminded persons. See *egocentricity, sociocentricity,* and *rationality*.

irrational emotions: Feelings based on unreasonable beliefs. Emotions are a natural part of human life. Irrational emotions reflect irrational beliefs or irrational responses to situations. They occur when our natural egocentricity leads us to behave in unproductive or unreasonable ways or when we are unsuccessful in getting our way (irrationally). Critical thinkers consistently work to diminish the power of irrational emotions in their life. See *rational emotions, emotions, emotional intelligence,* and *human mind*.

logical: Reasoning in accordance with the principles of logic; reasonable; to be expected; based on earlier or otherwise known statements, events, or conditions; consistent. This concept is an essential intellectual standard, and can be used in a relatively narrow sense (as in consistent), or in a broader sense (as in reasonable). The critical thinker routinely attempts to meet this standard, by asking questions such as: Is this conclusion logical? Is there a more reasonable or logical interpretation? Is this a logical inference given the data we have available to us? Is our position sound? See *reasonable*.

perspective: The faculty of seeing all the relevant data in logical relationship with one another, and with a broad view; seeing information, data, experiences in meaningful relationship with one another; a way of regarding situations or topics; a mental view or prospect; subjective evaluation. Note that there are at least two distinct uses of the term "perspective." One focuses on seeing things in a clear relationship with one another, in an integrated way, leading to a broad view (such as, "She is a person we can always count on to have a broad perspective," or "Keep things in perspective"). A second use refers to the particular mental view or logic from which one is approaching situations, ideas, and so on. All thought comes from some perspective, from some set of interrelated beliefs that form a logic in the mind of the thinker. This is the angle through which experiences are formed and new situations are viewed. We often give names to the direction from which we are thinking about something. For example, we might look at something politically or scientifically, poetically or philosophically. We might look at something conservatively or liberally, religiously or secularly. We might look at something from a cultural or a financial perspective, or both. Once we understand how people approach a question or topic (their comprehensive perspective), we can usually better understand the logic of their thinking as an organized whole. We can also better understand their point of view. See *point of view* and *world view*.

point of view: The precise place from which you view something; a mental position from which things are viewed; what you are looking at and how you are seeing it. Human thought is relational and selective. It is impossible to understand any person, event, or phenomenon from every vantage point simultaneously. Our purposes often control how we see things. Critical thinking requires that we take this into account when analyzing and assessing thinking. This is not to say that human thought is incapable of truth and objectivity, but only that human truth, objectivity, and insight are limited and partial, not total and absolute. By reasoning within a point of view, then, we mean that our thinking inevitably has some specific focus or orientation. Our thinking is focused on something from some angle. Our point of view is embedded in our perspective, but the term "perspective" is often used in a broader sense. We might look at a presidential candidate from a "liberal" perspective. But the point of view from which we see the candidate tends to be more specific, as in seeing this candidate as violating the principles of the liberal party (thus "looking at" this candidate and "seeing" him or her in the following way…). Skilled reasoners keep in mind that people have different points of view, especially on controversial issues, consistently articulate other points of view and reason from within those points of view to adequately understand them, seek other viewpoints (especially when the issue is one they believe in passionately), confine their monological reasoning to problems that are clearly monological, recognize when they are most likely to be prejudiced, and approach problems and issues with a richness of vision and an appropriately broad point of view. Unskilled reasoners do not credit alternative reasonable viewpoints, cannot see issues from points of view that are significantly different from their own; cannot reason with empathy from alien points of view, can sometimes give other points of view when the issue is not emotionally charged but cannot do so for issues about which they feel strongly, confuse multilogical with monological issues; insist that there is only one frame of reference within which a given multilogical question must be decided, are unaware of their own prejudices, and reason from within inappropriately narrow or superficial points of view. See *perspective, worldview,* and *elements of reasoning.*

precision: The quality of being specific, definite, detailed; exact measurement. Precision is an essential intellectual standard, and generally has two distinct meanings: exact to the necessary level of detail, or accuracy of measurement. In everyday reasoning, thinking might be precise; that is, detailed, and yet not be accurate, as in true. For example, you might say that the average person needs 356,453.9876 calories every day, being highly exact in the number of calories needed. But, though exact (precise in the first sense), this answer would not be true (precise in the second sense). Accuracy tends to play a role in precision where mathematical measurement is the focus. Precision, as in exactness, is important when details are necessary for reasoning through a problem or issue. The problem, issue, or question determines the level of precision needed. See *accurate* and *intellectual standards*.

purpose: Object, aim, goal, end in view; something one is hoping to accomplish. All reasoning has a purpose. In other words, when humans think about the world, we do not do so randomly but, rather, in line with our goals, desires, needs, and values. Our thinking is an integral part of a patterned way of acting in the world; and we act, even in simple matters, with some set of ends in view. To understand someone's thinking—including our own—we must understand the functions it serves, what it is about, the direction it is moving, and the ends that make sense of it. Raising human goals and desires to the level of conscious realization is an important part of critical thinking. Accordingly, critical thinkers take the time to state their purpose clearly, distinguish it from related purposes, and periodically remind themselves of their purpose to determine whether they are straying from it. Further, they adopt realistic purposes and goals, choose significant purposes and goals, choose goals and purposes that are consistent with one other, adjust their thinking regularly to their purpose, and choose purposes that are fairminded (considering the desires and rights of others equally with their own desires and rights). Conversely, uncritical thinkers are often unclear about their central purpose. They oscillate between different, sometimes contradictory, purposes. Moreover, they lose track of their fundamental object or goal, adopt unrealistic purposes, set unrealistic goals, adopt trivial purposes and goals as if they were significant, inadvertently negate their own purposes, fail to monitor their thinking for inconsistent goals, fail to adjust their thinking to their purpose, and choose purposes that are self-serving at the expense of others' needs and desires. See *elements of reasoning*.

question: A problem or matter open to discussion or inquiry; something that is asked, as in seeking to learn or gain knowledge. Humans are inherently purposeful. And integral to our purposes are questions that (hopefully) guide our thinking to the fulfillment of those purposes. The question at issue determines the intellectual task at hand. It determines the direction of our thinking. For example, the question determines the information needed to answer it. The question illuminates the viewpoints relevant to answering it. The question points to complexities in the issues being addressed (that need to be reasoned through). Accordingly, critical thinkers are clear about the question they are trying to settle, can re-express a question in a variety of ways, can break a question into subquestions, routinely distinguish questions of different types, distinguish significant from trivial questions, distinguish relevant questions from irrelevant ones, are sensitive to the assumptions built into the questions they ask, and distinguish questions they can answer from questions they can't. Uncritical thinkers, on the other hand, are often unclear about the question they are asking, express questions vaguely, find questions difficult to reformulate clearly, are unable to break down the questions they are asking, confuse questions of different types, confuse trivial questions with significant ones, confuse irrelevant questions with relevant ones, often ask loaded questions, and try to answer questions they are not in a position to answer. See *elements of reasoning*.

rational/rationality: Being guided by the intellect (rather than emotions), or having to do with reason; being consistent with or based on logic; that which conforms to principles of good reasoning, is sensible, shows good judgment, is consistent, logical, relevant, and sound. In everyday discourse, there are at least three different common uses of the term "rational" or "rationality." One refers to a person's general ability to think well. A second refers to a person's ability to use his intellect to achieve his purposes (irrespective of whether or not these purposes are ethically justified). A third refers to one's commitment to think and act only in ways that are intellectually and ethically justified. Behind these three uses lie these distinctions: skilled thinker, sophistic thinker, and Socratic thinker. In the first use, we mark the skills only of the thinker. In the second, we mark the skills used "self-ishly" (as the Sophists of old). In the third, we mark the skills used fairmindedly (as Socrates did). Critical thinkers, in the strong sense, are concerned with developing their capacities to reason with skill while also respecting the rights and needs of others. They are fair-minded in the use of their intellectual skills. See *intellectual virtues, strong-sense critical thinkers,* and *weak-sense critical thinkers.*

rational emotions (or rational passions): The affective dimension of skilled reason and critical thought. Emotions are an integral part of human life. Whenever we reason, there is always some emotion linked with our thoughts. Rational emotions are those connected with reasonable thought and action. R. S. Peters (1973)[21] explained the significance of "rational passions" as follows:

> "There is, for instance, the hatred of contradictions and inconsistencies, together with the love of clarity and hatred of confusion without which words could not be held to relatively constant meanings and testable rules and generalizations stated. A reasonable man cannot, without some special explanation, slap his sides with delight or express indifference if he is told that what he says is confused, incoherent, and perhaps riddled with contradictions. Reason is the antithesis of arbitrariness. In its operation it is supported by the appropriate passions which are mainly negative in character—the hatred of irrelevance, special pleading, and arbitrary fiat. The more developed emotion of indignation is aroused when some excess of arbitrariness is perpetuated in a situation where people's interests and claims are at stake. The positive side of this is the passion for fairness and impartial consideration of claims…A man who is prepared to reason must feel strongly that he must follow the arguments and decide things in terms of where they lead. Insofar as thoughts about persons enter his head, they should be tinged with the respect which is due to another who, like himself, may have a point of view which is worth considering, who may have a glimmering of the truth

21. Peters, R. S. (1973). *Reason and Compassion.* London: Routledge & Kegan Paul.

which has so far eluded himself. A person who proceeds in this way, who is influenced by such passions, is what we call a reasonable man." See *human mind, emotions,* and *irrational emotions.*

rational self: Human character and nature to the extent that we seek to base our beliefs and actions on good reasoning and evidence; the capacity of humans to think and behave in a reasonable manner (in contrast to thinking and behaving egocentrically). Each of us has both a "rational" and "irrational" self, a reasonable side and an unreasonable side. Although the irrational or egocentric side functions naturally, without cultivation, critical thinking is essential to the development of one's "rational self." Put another way, our rational capacities do not develop themselves. They aren't automatic in the mind, but must be developed by us. Present societies do not tend to cultivate rational persons, but rather (perhaps inadvertently) tend to encourage egocentric and sociocentric thought. See *rational, critical society, egocentricity,* and *sociocentricity.*

rationalize: To ascribe one's acts, opinions, and so on, to causes that seem (on the surface) reasonable and valid but that are not the true causes (while the real reasons are either unconscious, or seemingly less creditable or agreeable); to make rational or conformable to reason; to employ reason; think in a rational or rationalistic manner. Note that there are two distinctly different uses of the term "to rationalize." One is synonymous with thinking rationally or reasonably. The other is a defense mechanism commonly used by the human mind to keep something hidden, either from oneself or others. In this second use, to rationalize is to give reasons that "sound good," but are not one's actual reasons. Rationalization, in this second sense, is often used in situations where one is pursuing one's vested interests while trying to maintain the appearance of high ethical purpose. Politicians, for instance, after receiving large donations from special interest groups and then supporting these groups with votes or committee action, routinely rationalize their behavior, implying that they are acting from high motives when most likely the reverse is true. Those who held slaves often asserted that slavery was justified because slaves were like children and had to be treated as such. Rationalization, again in this second sense, is a defense mechanism that enables people to get what they want without having to face the fact that they are operating from selfish motives. Rationalizations enable people to keep their actual motives beneath the level of consciousness. They then can sleep peacefully at night while behaving unethically by day. Critical thinkers recognize the pernicious role that rationalization plays, or can play, in human thought and action. They realize that all of us rationalize our behavior at times, and that we must therefore work to diminish its frequency and power in our own thought and lives. See *defense mechanisms*.

reasonable: Adhering to reason or sound judgment; logical; governed by rational thought. An important macro-intellectual standard is that of being reasonable. A reasonable person is one who considers evidence without prejudice and routinely reaches sound, defensible, logical conclusions. The question of whether one is meeting the intellectual standard of "being reasonable" is given in context. That which is required for reasonability in one context might greatly differ from that which is considered reasonable in another. A reasonable conception of evolution is different from a reasonable approach to tennis practice. To meet the standard of "being reasonable," it is necessary to meet other intellectual standards as well, because reasonability is a "macro-intellectual standard" rather than a "micro-intellectual standard." For example, a reasonable interpretation of raw data in a study will entail the use of justifiable assumptions and concepts; it will require a clear question at issue; it will require a logical drawing of conclusions; and so forth. Moreover we might speak of a reasonable act in a narrow sense, or a reasonable person in a broader sense. An unreasonable person might, on occasion, behave reasonably. A reasonable person might, on occasion, behave unreasonably. At the highest level, a reasonable person embodies the intellectual virtues on a daily basis. See *intellectual standards* and *intellectual virtues*.

reasoning: The mental processes of those who reason; the process of forming conclusions, judgments, or inferences from facts, observations, hypotheses; the evidence or arguments used in this process.

By reasoning, we mean making sense of something by giving it some meaning in your mind. Almost all thinking is part of our sense-making activities. We hear scratching at the door and think, "It's the dog." We see dark clouds in the sky and think, "It looks like rain." Some of this activity operates at a subconscious level (for example, all of the sights and sounds about me have meaning for me without my explicitly noticing they do). Most of our reasoning is quite unspectacular. Our reasoning tends to become explicit to us only when it is challenged by someone and we have to defend it. ("Why do you say that Jack is obnoxious? I thought he was quite pleasant.") We take command of our reasoning when we understand that all reasoning entails component parts that can and should be regularly examined for quality. In other words, whenever we reason, we reason for a purpose within a point of view based on assumptions leading to implications and consequences. We use concepts, ideas, and theories to interpret data, facts, and experiences (information) to answer questions, solve problems, and resolve issues. The elements of reasoning (such as purpose, question, information, concepts, inferences, assumptions, implications, and point of view) are implicit in our thinking whenever we reason. Critical thinkers are aware of this, and routinely work to bring these parts of thinking to the conscious level to assess them for quality. See *elements of reasoning*.

relevant: Bearing upon or directly related to the matter at hand or question at issue; applicability to social issues. Relevance, in its most widely used form, is an essential intellectual standard focused on the extent to which something bears upon something else. People often have problems sticking to an issue and distinguishing information that bears on a problem from information that does not. Sensitivity to relevance, in this broad sense, is best developed with deliberate practice—practice distinguishing relevant from irrelevant data, evaluating or judging relevance, and arguing for and against the relevance of facts. A second use of the term refers to whether, and to what extent, something is applicable to social issues or life situations. Students will often, in studying a subject, question the relevance of the topic to their lives. Though they have every right to do so, they often claim that a topic is irrelevant to them simply because they are not motivated to learn it. As students develop intellectual skills and fairmindedness, they progressively come to see more and more topics, issues, concepts, and subjects as relevant to living rationally and fully; and they do this in virtue of their own independent thought. See *intellectual standards*.

self-deception: The natural human (egocentric) tendency to deceive oneself about one's true motivations, character, or identity. This phenomenon is so common to humans that the human species might well be defined "the self-deceiving animal." All of the defense mechanisms are facilitated by this egocentric tendency. Through self-deception, humans are able to ignore unpleasant realities and problems in their thinking and behavior. Self-deception reinforces self-righteousness and intellectual arrogance. It enables us to pursue selfish interests while disguising our motives as altruistic or reasonable. Through self-deception, humans "justify" flagrantly unethical acts, policies, and practices. All humans engage in self-deception— but not to the same degree. Overcoming self-deception through critical thinking is a fundamental goal of strong sense critical thinking. See *egocentricity, defense mechanisms, rational self,* and *intellectual virtues*.

selfish interest: What is perceived to be useful to oneself without regard for the rights and needs of others. To be selfish is to seek what one desires without due consideration for others. Being interested in one's own welfare is one thing; trampling on the rights of others in the pursuit of one's own desires is another. As fundamentally egocentric creatures, humans naturally pursue their selfish interests. We frequently use rationalization and other forms of self-deception to disguise our true motives and the true character of what we are doing. To develop as fairminded critical thinkers is to work actively to diminish the power of one's native selfishness without sacrificing any legitimate concerns for one's welfare and long-term good. See *egocentricity, self-deception, rational self,* and *intellectual virtues*.

sociocentricity: The belief in the inherent superiority of one's own group or culture; a tendency to judge alien people, groups, or cultures from the perspective of one's own group. As social animals, humans cluster together. Indeed, the survival of the human species depends upon a lengthy rearing process so that all humans survive, in the first instance, because they are cared for within a group. Accordingly, children learn from an early age to think within the logic of the group. This is required for their "acceptance" in the group. As part of this socialization process, they (largely uncritically) absorb group ideologies. Sociocentricity is based on the assumption that one's own social group is inherently and self-evidently superior to all others. When a group or society sees itself as superior, and so considers its views as correct or as the only reasonable or justifiable views and when a group perceives all of its actions as justified, it has a tendency to think closed-mindedly. Dissent and doubt are considered disloyal and are rejected. Few people recognize the sociocentric nature of much of their thought. Sociocentric thought is connected with the term "ethnocentricity," although ethnocentricity is often used more narrowly to refer to sociocentric thought within an ethnic group. See *egocentricity*.

stages of critical thinking development: A theory of development focusing on the stages of progression in critical thinking skills, abilities, and dispositions; presupposes internal motivation on the part of the thinker to develop as a fairminded critical thinker (originally conceptualized by Linda Elder, and then expanded by Linda Elder and Richard Paul.[22] People generally develop within any complex skill area through stages, beginning at a low level of skill and slowly progressing toward higher and higher levels of accomplishment. The stages of critical thinking are as follows:

Stage One: The Unreflective Thinker (the thinker is unaware of problems in her thinking)

Stage Two: The Challenged Thinker (the thinker is faced with significant problems in her thinking)

Stage Three: The Beginning Thinker (the thinker tries to improve, but without regular practice)

---

22. See Elder, L. and Paul, R. (2012). *Critical Thinking: Tools for Taking Charge of Your Learning and Your Life*, 3rd ed. Boston, MA: Pearson Education.

Stage Four: The Practicing Thinker (the thinker regularly practices and begins to advance accordingly)

Stage Five: The Advanced Thinker (the thinker becomes committed to lifelong practice and has cultivated intellectual virtues to a high degree)

Stage Six: The Accomplished Thinker (intellectual virtues have become second nature to the thinker and she routinely displays them within all the important domains of her life [formerly "Master Thinker"].)

This theory is based on the following assumptions: (1) that there are predictable stages through which every person who develops as a fairminded critical thinker passes, (2) that passage from one stage to the next depends on a necessary level of commitment on the part of an individual to develop as a critical thinker, is not automatic, and is unlikely to take place "subconsciously," (3) that one develops greater commitment to critical thinking as one moves through the stages, and (4) that regression is possible in development (and actually quite common). People are critical thinkers, in the fullest sense of the term, only if they display critical thinking abilities and dispositions in all, or most, of the dimensions of their lives (for example, as a parent, citizen, consumer, lover, friend, learner, and professional). Though we recognize that there are many forms and manifestations of critical thinking, we are focused in these stages only on those people who develop as critical thinkers in the strong sense. We exclude from our concept of the critical thinker (in terms of the stages) those who think critically in only one dimension of their lives. We do so because the quality of one's life is dependent on high quality reasoning in all domains of one's life, not simply in one dimension. The primary reasons why people fail to develop as critical thinkers are: they fail to recognize that thinking, left to itself, is likely to contain flaws (so they never attempt to intervene in their thinking in a systematic way); they fall victim to native egocentric thought (and its self-deceptive tendencies); and they remain dominated by native sociocentric thought. See *intellectual virtues, strong-sense critical thinkers, egocentricity,* and *sociocentricity.*

strong-sense critical thinkers: Fairminded critical thinkers; skilled thinkers characterized predominantly by the following traits: (1) the ability and tendency to question deeply one's own views; (2) the ability and tendency to reconstruct sympathetically and imaginatively the strongest versions of viewpoints and perspectives opposed to one's own; (3) the ability and tendency to reason dialectically (multilogically) in such a way as to determine when one's own point of view is at its weakest and when an opposing point of view is at its strongest; and (4) the ability and propensity to change one's thinking when the evidence would require it, without regard to one's own selfish or vested interests. Strong-sense critical thinkers are fundamentally concerned with reasoning at the highest level of skill, considering all the important available evidence, and respecting all relevant viewpoints. Their thought and behavior is characterized primarily by intellectual virtues or habits of mind. They avoid being blinded by their own viewpoints. They recognize the framework of assumptions and ideas upon which their own viewpoints are based. They realize the necessity of putting their assumptions and ideas to the test of the strongest objections that can be leveled against them. Most importantly, they can be moved by reason; that is, they are willing to abandon their own ideas when other ideas prove more reasonable or valid. Teaching for strong-sense critical thinking entails routinely encouraging students to explicate, understand, and critique their deepest prejudices, biases, and misconceptions, thereby discovering and contesting their egocentric and sociocentric tendencies (for only when we do so can we hope to develop as fairminded persons). Regularly thinking dialogically about important and personal issues is necessary for developing strong-sense critical thinking. If critical thinking is taught simply as atomic skills separate from the empathic practice of entering into points of view that students are fearful of or hostile toward, they will simply find additional means of rationalizing prejudices and preconceptions, or convincing people that their point of view is the correct one. They will be transformed from vulgar or naïve thinkers to sophisticated (but not strong-sense) critical thinkers. See *intellectual virtues, fairmindedness,* and *weak-sense critical thinkers*.

unconscious thought: Thinking that occurs without awareness; ideas, experiences, assumptions, and so on, beneath the level
of awareness but that have a pronounced influence on behavior (and
on conscious thoughts); thoughts lying below the level of perception
and not easily raised into consciousness; thoughts we are unaware of,
and which we would rather avoid explicitly perceiving. Two distinctly
different uses of this term are relevant for our purposes here. The
first use is equated with the term "subconscious thought." It simply
refers to thoughts in our minds that we are not explicitly aware of at
any given moment, but from which we have no "need" to hide. The
second use refers to suppressed thoughts—thoughts in our minds we
are unaware of that influence our conscious thoughts and behavior,
and which we are for some reason motivated to avoid recognizing.
These might be painful or unpleasant "experiences," or they might
be dysfunctional patterns of thought—such as rationalization or other
forms of self-deception. Much human thinking is unconscious. It is
quite common for people to be guided by ideas, assumptions, and
perspectives that exist in their minds, but of which they have little
or no awareness. All egocentric and sociocentric thoughts have some
unconscious dimension to them because these thoughts can't stand
the light of day. In other words, if we were to face the fact that these
thoughts were operating in our thinking, we would be "forced" to
deal with them. This might require us to give up something we hold
dear. Any thoughts that we cannot openly "own" have an unconscious
dimension. To the extent that thoughts are unconscious in the mind,
we have little chance of analyzing and assessing them. We have little
chance of exploring how they influence our thoughts and behavior.
Critical thinkers are aware of this, and therefore routinely work to
bring unconscious thoughts to the level of consciousness in order to
examine them for quality. See *defense mechanisms, egocentricity,
self-deception,* and *sociocentricity.*

vested interest: Promoting personal advantage, usually at the
expense of others; group pursuit of collective goals, exerting influence that enables the group to profit, often at the expense of others. One natural implication of sociocentric thought is the problem of

group vested interest. Every group potentially falls prey to this native human tendency—to seek more for its own group at the expense of others. For example, many groups that lobby Congress do so to gain money, power, and advantage for themselves by provisions in law that specially favors their group. The term "vested interest" classically contrasts with the term "public interest." A group that lobbies Congress in the public interest is not seeking to gain special advantage for a comparative few but, rather, protection for the majority. Preserving the quality of the air is a public interest. Building cheaper cars by using second-rate material is a vested interest (it makes more money for car manufacturers). The term "vested interest" has been largely replaced with the term "special interest" by those seeking vested interests, because they do not want their real agenda to come to light. By advancing the notion that all groups are simply seeking to protect and expand their special interest, these groups hope to place their selfish agenda on the same footing with agendas in the public interest. See *selfish interest* and *sociocentric thought*.

weak-sense critical thinkers: Those who use the skills, abilities, and to some extent, the traits of critical thinking to serve their selfish interests; unfair or unethical critical thinkers. Weak-sense, or unethical critical thinkers, have the following pronounced tendencies: (1) They do not hold themselves or those with whom they ego-identify to the same intellectual standards to which they hold opponents. (2) They do not reason empathically within points of view or frames of reference with which they disagree. (3) They tend to think monologically (within one narrow perspective). (4) They do not genuinely accept, though they might verbally espouse, the values of fairminded critical thinking. (5) They use intellectual skills selectively and self-deceptively to foster and serve their selfish interests at the expense of truth. 6) They use critical thinking skills to identify flaws in the reasoning of others and sophisticated arguments to refute others' arguments before giving those arguments due consideration. (7) They routinely justify their irrational thinking through highly sophisticated rationalizations. (8) They are highly skilled at manipulation. The opposite is *strong-sense critical thinkers*. See also *egocentricity, irrational,* and *rationalization*.

world view: A way of looking at and interpreting the world, based largely on our assumptions and conceptual orientation. Each of us has a belief system, or world view, through which we interpret events, situations, experiences, people, nature, and so on. This world view changes to some extent over time, and in some cases, is enriched as we grow and age. And it is the beginning place for thinking in new contexts. In other words, we develop our world view over time, taking in the ideas of those around us, deciding which ideas to accept and which to reject; and we bring our world view with us to every new situation and circumstance. Thus, we have a belief system, or a mental map of ideas, assumptions, and so on, through which we experience everything in the world. And most of us are largely trapped within our world view. Consequently we see our way of thinking as the right way to think, not as one possible way to think. Most of us have a world view that is largely sociocentric, based on uncritically accepted views and ideas of the groups that have influenced us. For instance, most of us are trapped in nationalistic, patriotic, and jingoistic orientations. We see our country as the best and brightest. We see our values and ideals as superior to all others. This nationalistic perspective is a significant part of our world view. We rarely analyze or assess it. The idea of becoming a citizen of the world, being just as concerned with the rights and needs of people in other countries as those in our own, doesn't occur to us, trapped as we are in our sociocentric orientation. Besides having a global world view, we all have internalized multiple subordinate world views. Some are gender-based; some are economically based; some are culturally based, and so on. In all likelihood, there are multiple contradictions that exist within and among these subordinate views without our knowledge. Critical thinking challenges us to face our contradictions and work through them until our belief systems have intellectual and ethical integrity. In most schooling today, little is done to help students grasp how they are viewing the world and how those views determine the character of their experience, their interpretations, and their conclusions about events and persons. Consequently most students have no notion that they have a world view and that this world view can be molded. In learning critical thinking in a strong sense, we make it a priority to discover our own world view and open-mindedly think within the views of others. See also *point of view, perspective, world view,* and *sociocentric thought.*

References

The following references were used in formulating many of the brief definitions in this glossary:

- *Online Etymology Dictionary.* Retrieved January 20, 2009, from Dictionary.com website: http://dictionary.reference.com/browse.
- *Random House Unabridged Dictionary.* Random House, Inc. 2006. Retrieved January 20, 2009, from Dictionary.com Unabridged (v 1.1).
- *The American Heritage® Dictionary of the English Language,* Fourth Edition. Retrieved January 19, 2008, from Dictionary .com.
- *Webster's New World College Dictionary,* Fourth Edition, Wiley Publishing, 2007.
- *Webster's Revised Unabridged Dictionary.* Retrieved January 20, 2009, from Dictionary.com website: http://dictionary.reference.com/browse.
- WordNet™ 3.0. Retrieved January 20, 2009, from Dictionary .com website: http://dictionary.reference.com/browse.

Index

FT Press

FINANCIAL TIMES

In an increasingly competitive world, it is quality
of thinking that gives an edge—an idea that opens new
doors, a technique that solves a problem, or an insight
that simply helps make sense of it all.

We work with leading authors in the various arenas
of business and finance to bring cutting-edge thinking
and best-learning practices to a global market.

It is our goal to create world-class print publications
and electronic products that give readers
knowledge and understanding that can then be
applied, whether studying or at work.

To find out more about our business
products, you can visit us at www.ftpress.com.